HAUNTED SEGUIN

HAUNTED SEGUIN

ERIN O. WALLACE

Haunted
America

Published by Haunted America
A Division of The History Press
Charleston, SC 29403
www.historypress.net

Copyright © 2014 by Erin O. Wallace
All rights reserved

First published 2014

ISBN 978.1.5402.0788.3

Library of Congress CIP data applied for

This book is dedicated to Pearl E. Lacroix Goldate (1922–1991). Pearl (known to the locals in St. Tammany Parish as the Peacock Lady) believed that every building was a shell of the owners' lives who lived there, giving it a soul and an important role in history. This unusual belief inspired me to see old buildings beyond the walls that held them together and wonder more about the lives of the people who once resided there. Pearl held dear to her heart the belief that every building's history has a right to survive, even if only one person cares to remember. After her passing, it was her strong conviction that encouraged me to continue her quest in transforming her beloved Fairview Riverside Otis House into a Louisiana state museum. When an old building is demolished, the history of the people who lived among it is lost as well. The quote "If only these walls could talk" is truer than most people wish to believe. They actually can speak, if we only listen with our eyes, hearts and minds, not just our ears. All it takes is one person to devote time to uncovering a building's words by listening to locals and researching archives and libraries. Then you become the building's voice, do the talking for it and share what stories have been found. Without a doubt, although Pearl is no longer here, I am certain she had a hand in guiding me to continue to speak for these silent buildings. I am confident she still stands by my side in saving forgotten historic buildings, for together we just rescued another.

The 1840s Magnolia Hotel before restoration around the late 1980s. *Photo courtesy of Texas Most Endangered Places, Preservation Texas.*

CONTENTS

THE GHOST BARRICADE

Seguin is one of the most unique and fascinating cities in Texas. Besides its labeling in history as the "city built of concrete" and "mother of concrete," it is also a quaint town known for having endured Indian attacks, assaults by the Mexican army, the invasion of Northern soldiers during Reconstruction, the Great Depression years, flood and drought—and that is just to name a few. Yet community members have always rallied together to help one another and refused to allow their small town to fade away like so many others. Not only is this a tight knit community with many descendants of the original founders still living there, but it is also an area considered to be one of the most haunted places in this great state. It has been described as "the city whose citizens refuse to leave, even after death." Of course, it is a beautiful place worthy of the desire to remain even in the afterlife, but some believe this desire is due to the town's man-made surroundings, known to the paranormal realm as the "ghost barricade."

This unsuspecting small frontier community was once the hub for testing out a specially patented material known as limecrete invented by the highly creative physician and chemist Dr. John Esten Park, who moved to Seguin in the late 1840s. Park used crews of male slaves to dig caliches and gravel on location and then brought water and sand from the streams nearby for his experiment. The items were then mixed with ash, clay and lime, which was produced from the Hill Country limestone brought in from San Marcos by wagons. This procedure demanded extremely skilled labor to get the proper quantities just right, or the limecrete would not set

"Historic American Buildings Survey, Marvin Eickenroht, Photographer March 1, 1934 VIEW FROM SOUTHWEST. Colonel Joshua Young House, 704 Mill Avenue, Seguin, Guadalupe County, TX." *Library of Congress, Prints & Photographs Division, HABS HABS TEX,94-SEGUI,1—1.*

properly. The end results were immensely strong limecrete walls that were firmly insulated, fireproof and, unexpectedly, ghost lures. Seguin quickly became known for its extraordinary concentration of concrete buildings and was labeled "the city made of concrete." Astonishingly, at the time of Dr. Park's death in 1872, Seguin had a general population of no more than one thousand people with almost ninety limecrete buildings, plus numerous other structures such as animal pens, fences, cisterns and the now very famous limecrete barricade.

During 1840, Seguin even used Dr. Park's limecrete invention to build the now famous wall that encircles the small city. This innovative decision would eventually distinguish Seguin as the only walled city in Texas. The limecrete wall was primarily built for protection from Indian attacks and the Mexican army. It was then gratefully used to separate Seguin from a short-lived town called Guadalupe City. This town was considered to be a very unruly area known for its rowdy saloons and bawdyhouses. Later, after the two cities merged, the wall helped keep wildlife and livestock from eating the gardens of the locals. Unbeknownst to the citizens of Seguin at the time of construction, their specially made limecrete is now believed by many to be a conduit for spirits. This particular mixture has been branded by the paranormal realm for attracting and even energizing spirits wishing to make their presence known. It wasn't until the arrival of the railroad in

"Historic American Buildings Survey, William C. Kleine, Photographer February 10, 1934 VIEW FROM NORTHEAST. Colonel Joshua Young House, 704 Mill Avenue, Seguin, Guadalupe County, TX." *Library of Congress, Prints & Photographs Division, HABS HABS TEX,94-SEGUI,1—3.*

1875, which brought in lumber and bricks, that the use of limecrete finally came to a halt. Today, only a handful of the limecrete relics still survive in Seguin, such as the 1840 Magnolia Hotel and the Sebastopol House and, of course, the ghost barricade. Only portions of these relics remain, but they are still energizing the spirits. These scarce limecrete buildings and wall now stand as a monument to Dr. Park's clever use of local resources and his ingenious invention. They are also hushed barriers keeping in certain spirits that wish to remain, while they continue to draw in those who simply seek a safe environment. This most definitely explains Seguin's vast hauntings and its designation as one of "One of Texas's Most Haunted Cities." If you sincerely seek paranormal activity, spend a day or night in the historic area of Seguin—if you dare. One word of advice, though: be sure you exit the city limits alive, or the limecrete ghost barricade just might make certain you remain for all of eternity, whether or not you want to.

ACKNOWLEDGEMENTS

This publication of *Haunted Seguin* was by no means an individual task. It was a story that had been in the making for nearly five years when I first began this paranormal ride. Had it not been for all who assisted me along this journey, it would never had been accomplished, and for this I wish to express my deepest gratitude. So many caring volunteers made this experience thrilling, fulfilling and memorable. First and foremost, I want to personally thank everyone who allowed their historical buildings to be included in this book. Their hospitality, entrance into their buildings and personal accounts offered invaluable assistance to the project. I owe an enormous group hug to my paranormal family called the "Ripcrew," the Researching Investigating Paranormal (RIP) team, whose serious dedication to this endeavor gave crucial evidence to this work. This team—consisting of founder Robbie Prince, co-founder Wiley Uzzell, April Prince, Margie Uzzell, Shannon Autrey, Jennifer Autrey and Chris Slaughter—tirelessly worked around my schedule, for which I am obliged. They gave up valuable family time to make certain this book received the evidence needed to be as accurate as possible. Very special thanks go to talented photographer Megan Foster for the book's amazing cover photo and author Janice Woods Windle for being an immense inspiration without her even knowing it. To author Andrea Perron, I want to deeply thank you for saying just the right words that I desperately needed to hear when I was beginning to doubt my path. Also, the knowledge and guidance from the extraordinary historian E. John Gesick Jr. and the photos from the Seguin-Guadalupe County Heritage

Right: Author and owner of the Magnolia Hotel Erin O. Wallace and her husband, Jim Ghedi. *Photo by Megan Foster.*

Below: The Ripcrew Paranormal Team. *Top row, left to right*: Chris Slaughter and Robbie Prince; *bottom row, left to right*: Wiley Uzzell, Jennifer Autrey, Shannon Autrey, April Prince and Margie Uzzell. *Photo by Megan Foster.*

Museum helped bring the city's history in the book to life. I want to deeply thank the citizens of Seguin for openly sharing their own haunted stories and the thousands of Facebook friends who inspired me on a daily basis. To my mother-in-law, best friend and cheerleader, Billie Jo Witcher Ghedi, who stepped in to support me when others walked away, thank you just doesn't seem enough. A tremendous hug and thank-you goes out to my sister, Maureen "Mickey" Cavin, for taking charge and great care of our family during the loss of our two family members just four months apart. She was our entire family's strength. To my two children, Jennifer "Jen" Lynn Mangiapane Coffey and Michael "Mike" Gerard Mangiapane; Michael's wife, Veronica "Roni" Zavala Mangiapane; and my granddaughter, Gabrielle "Gabby" Juliet Baudoin, I appreciate you all letting me bend your ears with my lengthy ghost and history stories every time we were together. I would have bust if I hadn't been allowed to share with someone. Finally, I am forever indebted to my high school sweetheart and now husband, James "Jim" William Ghedi, for his understanding, endless patience and encouragement when it was most required to keep me focused. He is my sanctuary and my rock when the world around me is turning upside down. I could not have completed this without him. This was an experience I will forever cherish and never forget.

Introduction

THE CITY BUILT BY TEXAS RANGERS

Following the Texas Revolution and the Runaway Scrape, available land in Gonzales had become scarce. This encouraged members of Mathew Caldwell's Gonzales Rangers to begin seeking a new area to start a city. The enormous walnut and oak orchards along the Walnut Branch Creek had become an enjoyable location for many of the Texas Rangers. It had been a gathering place for the Rangers during their guards against bandits and unscrupulous Indians and was used as a base camp by the Rangers since the early establishment of the Dewitt Colony. This pleasant camp had been located in the center of the 1831 Umphries Branch league.

With this in mind on August 12, 1838, three men founded a corporation, along with Joseph Martin, who owned the property, and laid out the plans for a town to be called Walnut Springs, about thirty-six miles from Gonzales. The men agreed to buy a portion of the Umphries Branch league to sell shares of the property for the objective of creating a new town. The original shareholders numbered thirty-three. Many of these investors' descendants still live in Seguin today. Most of these shareholders played a huge part in Seguin's future founding. They served proudly in either the Texas Militia during the Revolution or in the Texas army or were members of the invincible Texas Rangers. The original shareholders were James Campbell, Arthur Swift, William Killen, William Clinton, Henry B. King, Jeremiah Roberts, Barnett Randle, James A. Swift, Abraham Roberts, John R. King, James M. Day, Wilson Randle, Andrew Neill, P.C. Bell, W.A. Hall, Matthew Caldwell, Paschal Martin, French Smith, Michael Cody, H.G. Henderson, William

Historic Landmark sign in Seguin, Texas, for the Ranger Oaks. *Photo by author.*

Cody, Razia Sinclair, A. S. Emmett, Andrew J. Sowell, John H. Russell, M.S. Bebee, Miles G. Dikes, Kelley Mattheney, George W. Nichols, M.P. Woodhouse and Cyrus Crosby, plus two others whose names were unfortunately unreadable in the original documents of this transaction. There were forty-four shares available; thirty-three shares were sold, and eleven were reserved for Martin, who was allowed to dispose of them in any way he felt best. The new shares were drawn by a lottery, with the first choice of the lot location going to the man who drew the highest number. The man who drew lucky number forty-four was James Campbell, who picked the lot where the Magnolia Hotel still stands today.

On February 25, 1839, John R. King and James Campbell made a legal motion to have the town's name be changed to Seguin in honor of a true Texas patriot in their eyes, Juan Seguin.

While the newly named town of Seguin was being laid out one day in March 1840, over sixty Comanches arrived in San Antonio with a white woman, Matilda Lockhart, who had been kidnapped and badly brutalized. They proudly brought her in hopes of an exchange for a permanent peace treaty. Her horrible condition outraged the soldiers, and the plan quickly backfired. Seguin's Captain Caldwell and the other Rangers became so furious at the sight of Miss Lockhart and the story she told of fifteen other young women still held hostage that control of the meeting was lost, and a large number of the Comanches present were killed.

The remaining Comanche tribe's response to their gesture of a peaceful treaty's violation was intensely heated and tremendously deadly. The Comanches went on a slaughtering rampage throughout southeast Texas, murdering, scorching or harming anyone in sight. Ben McCulloch swiftly gathered his men from Seguin—along with Captain Caldwell's Rangers and Generals Felix Huston and Edward Burleson and their brave men—for a battle to end this deadly war with the Comanches. At Plum Creek, eighty Comanches were killed. With the men of Seguin's strength now having made an impression on the tribe, the Comanches never again attacked in such force, though they would remain a menace for many years.

Although they had subdued the Indians, things would not remain calm for long. On March 5, 1842, the disgruntled and shamed Santa Anna, along with his Mexican army, refused to admit defeat and ordered General Vasquez to invade Texas once again. With an army of 1,400 men, they had taken Goliad, Victoria and San Antonio and then symbolically raised the Mexican flag. Now the Mexican army was headed to Salado Creek. This would begin the creation of the famous legend of Texas Ranger captain John "Jack" Coffee Hays, who would lead the resistance forces on September 17, 1842. Hays and his men gallantly rode to the Salado Creek, and after an extremely well-planned strategy was put into place, the battle at Salado Creek was fought and won. This battle proved to be a significant victory for the Texans. From then on, Hays would become a familiar resident of Seguin. In 1843, Hays set up his historic Texas Ranger

Texas Rangers Co. A., 1910
(1) A.J.Sowell; (2)S.T.Townsend; (3) Charley Pace; (4)Joe Davenport; (5) S.Smiley; (6) A.R.Baker; (7) Robt.Speed; (8) Sam McKenzie; (9)Capt.J.J.Sanders;(10)Earl Yeary.

Copyright by the Leon Studio Collection of the Heritage Museum.

training station in Seguin. This would be where Hays would meet his beloved Susan Calvert, and they would later be married in Seguin's first hotel, the Magnolia Hotel, in 1847.

The years of 1838 to 1845 were hard on Seguin, but as this frontier town gained a foothold, settlers began to stream in. On the monumental date of December 29, 1845, President Polk signed the celebrated Texas Admissions Act, making Texas a part of the United States. This put Texas and its great people on an exciting new course, and Seguin would end up playing a significant role in the ongoing growth of Texas.

Though these years were draining on the young men of Seguin, the town continued to flourish. By early 1846, Seguin had its first stagecoach station; the route connected Gonzales to New Braunfels, and then it connected with the lines from East Texas and Louisiana. Seguin rapidly became a place to stop and shop for the flood of immigrants along their route from the ports of Galveston and Indianola to the German settlements of Fredericksburg and New Braunfels.

The period from 1846 to 1860 was Seguin's most productive and resourceful one. During this time, roads were planned out and stagecoach routes put in place. The city had a jail, post office, hotels, recreation events, clubs and organizations, as well as several newspapers. Technological innovations were achieved in construction and agricultural businesses, making Seguin a

"Historic American Buildings Survey, Arthur W. Stewart, Photographer April 29, 1936. Magnolia Hotel, 203 South Crockett Street, Seguin, Guadalupe County, TX." *Library of Congress, Prints & Photographs Division, HABS HABS TEX,-SEGUI,2—1.*

Front: "Way down south in the land of Cotton." *Back*: "Tuck's post card. Carte postale. Postkarte. By Appointment. 'Way down south in the land of cotton.' The most expensive process of cotton culture is the picking of it; despite various inventions, hand picking is the most satisfactory, and from 30 to 50 center a hundred-weight is paid men, women and children. 200 to 300 pounds of seed cotton is considered a good day's work; the fields are picked once in two or three weeks, and the season lasts about three months. Rapehel Truck and Sons' Series No. 2370, 'In the Land of Cotton.' Art Publishers to their majesties the king and queen. Photocromed in Saxony." *Author's private postcard collections.*

dynamic community until the coming of the dreadful Civil War. For the next twelve to fourteen years, courage was evident in many forms.

Many good men were lost while the women were left behind to run homes, farms and businesses and endure any news from the war. On June 19, 1865, a declaration proclaimed that all slaves were freed men. During the Reconstruction period, courage was shown by keeping personal values safe while publicly accepting the various federal commands that were often discriminatory. In 1867, the Freedman's Bureau settled in at the Davis home, where the Plaza Hotel stands today, directly across from Seguin's Market Square. A large company of Union soldiers were stationed in Seguin to implement the Reconstruction laws now in place. Rows upon rows of tents could be seen up and down the streets. The purpose of the Freedman's Bureau was to support the freed slaves in becoming accepted citizens in Seguin. Many had remained in Guadalupe County, taking the last names of their owners if they had been treated properly. Finally, the oldest railway in Texas, known as the Galveston, Harrisburg and San Antonio Railroad and chartered as the Buffalo Bayou, Brazos and Colorado Railway Company, erected the first Seguin train depot in 1876, which opened up new avenues

Photo of Magnolia Hotel at far right with the original jail in the center of picture around the early 1900s. *Picture courtesy of Heritage Museum.*

for Seguin. Though the railroad helped, it would not be until the 1880s that Seguin would be able to return to the economic success it had relished in the early 1850s.

After Reconstruction and into the 1900s, Seguin was full of peace and growth. It would receive electricity, telephones and a functioning water works. In 1912, an offer of fifteen acres and $20,000 from local businessmen of Seguin helped relocate an academy called the Lutheran College of Seguin, Texas, which was one building on a bare former cotton field, with 46 students. Today, it is called the Texas Lutheran University, with forty buildings on 184 acres serving over 1,400 students per semester.

By the early 1900s, Seguin had bakeries, groceries, cotton gins, flour mills, brick factories, hotels, blacksmiths, drummers (known as salesmen now), drugstores, opera houses, dry goods stores, stately homes, banks, saddleries, churches, private clubs, parks, saloons, swimming pools and organizations. Even during the 1920s, there was the great oil boom of the

Front: "Plaza Hotel, Seguin, Texas—1." *Back*: "The Plaza Hotel faced the beautiful Central park and plaza, where east breezes sway. The plaza is a modern fireproof hotel with up to date facilities. [Handwritten] Jan. 15 -43. How is every lady wrote Henry a letter before leaving home and will write you the first chance I get. Hope you all are enjoying the best of health. I am OK and the folks at home are well. Best Reganda Lenwood." Address: Mr. W.J. Howell. 346-5-Potl Dy. Granville, Ala. *Author's private postcard collections.*

Front: "Austin Street, Looking North, Seguin, Tex." *Back*: "Dear Aunt Hedwig, was extremely sorry to hear your father was so ill. I hope this will find him well again all ok. again. Had the children kased at the dance last night-they extremely enjoyed it. We are having a little better weather not I's been cold for ever so long. With love from all your niece, Lena Buene." Address: Miss Louis Forke Carlsbad N.M. *Author's private postcard collections.*

23

Front: "Old Main, Texas Lutheran College, Seguin, Texas." *Back*: "8/13/51 Dear Mom and Dad, My major is English and minor history. The only language I'll have is Greek. Across the hall is a Peterson from August-ana in Stamford. Swede. You are supposed to write me a ltter of permission to take smallpox shot. My address is just T.h.e. Seguin, Tex. Love, son." Sticker on sleeve: "Windows into the Past 1148N" *Author's private postcard collections.*

Front: "Texas Lutheran College, Seguin, Texas. 2a1317-N." *Back*: "Seguin was founded in 1838, and was named in honor Col. Juan N. Seguin, a patriot of the battle of San Jacinto. Its principal industries are pecans, cotton, oil, flour, dairy productions, and hydro-electric power generation. It is noted for its parks and municipally owned utilities. Genuine Curteich-Chicago C.T. American Art: Postcard (Reg. U.S. Pat. Off.)" *Author's private postcard collections.*

Front: "Seguin High School, Seguin, Texas. 2a1316-N." *Back*: "Genuine Curteich-Chicago C.T. American Art: Postcard (Reg. U.S. Pat. Off.)" *Author's private postcard collections.*

Plaza Hotel on right with Magnolia Hotel in center. *Copyright by the Leon Studio Collection of the Heritage Museum.*

Front: "Lutheran Church, Built 1913, Seguin, Tex." *Back*: "P.T. Photocrom. R-42991." *Author's private postcard collections.*

Front: "Swimming Pool, Max Starcke Park, seguin Texas. 9a68-N/." *Back*: "Seguin was founded in 1838, and was named in honor Col. Juan N. Seguin, a patriot of the battle of San Jacinto. Its principal industries are pecans, cotton, oil, flour, dairy productions, and hydro-electric power generation. It is noted for its parks and municipally owned utilities. Genuine Curteich-Chicago C.T. American Art: Postcard (Reg. U.S. Pat. Off.)" *Author's private postcard collections.*

Front: "Central Park, Seguin, Texas—2." *Back*: "Central Park has a multi-colored electric stone fountain, stone bandstand and a public comfort station and in this beautiful park will be found flower os all hues. [Handwritten] Hello Folks—We're just a few miles from San Antonio. It's been a wonderful trip along the Gulf of Mexico; It has been warm for here but chilly for us. Having breakfast now so as usual we're in a hurry—Lovel Smiths." Address: Mrs. Alyce B. Gravelle Mahnomen Minnestoa Star Route. *Author's private postcard collections.*

"'Main Street' Seguin, Texas. 'Gateway to Texas' Home of Texas Lutheran College, Max Starcke Park and Lake McQueeny. Photo by Wayne Craige. Wolcott & Sons, P.O. Box 1044, San Angelo, Texas 78901." Number in bottom right hand corner—S-70177. *Author's private postcard collections.*

Darst Creek Fields, only sixteen miles east of Seguin, which made for a profitable future.

Sadly, just like in every American city during wartime, Seguin's men would be called to duty in the battlefields of World War I, World War II, Korea and even Vietnam. Yet part of Seguin's honored legacy is rooted in quiet patriotism. This was reflected in the days of the Texas Revolution. The men, supported by their women, fought for the very freedom of their existence and the livelihood of their republic and state. Seguinites have served, been wounded and died in battle since the early 1830s up to the present day, and yet the city's strong bond and desire to continue to excel as a successful community is commendable. This is a city that has proven beyond a doubt that its citizens are just as tough and resilient as their ancestors. If Seguin's past is an example of what is in store, then the future looks bright. One cannot wait to see what lays ahead for this quaint yet enthusiastic and durable city.

Chapter 1

THE PALACE THEATRE

THE FOUR AWAKENED GHOSTS

Close your eyes for a moment and allow yourself to go back in time for a brief and delightful period. It is a hot summer's day in Texas as you eagerly walk up to a small glassed-in structure, greeted by a grinning person sensing your anticipation. You keenly announce to this smiling attendant your chosen make-believe destination. Curious about what excitement awaits you, you are handed a ticket permitting you to venture off into a world of imagination. You then push open a heavy glass door and are met by the delightfully cold breeze of an air conditioner. You stroll down a short pathway that leads you into a large, dimly lit room with the cheerful sounds of fidgety and excited people all around. As you squint your eyes to adjust to the light, you can hear the occasional slurp of a soda with a giggle afterward. Continuing on your journey down this path to your unknown destiny, the smells of buttery popcorn, salty peanuts and sour dill pickles make your mouth water. After searching for that perfectly located empty seat, you plop down and lean back in the chair. Needing one more adjustment to make you feel all nestled in, you prop both feet up on the seat in front of you. Then, before you know it, someone comes by with a long stick to sharply swat your feet down.

Bet you can guess where you are by now. It is an old school indoor theater. In this particular case, you have been transported inside the historical Palace Theatre, located at 314 South Austin Street. What separates this story from that of any other timeworn theater are the long-term employees who monitor the audience. These staff members are dedicated, tireless, highly devoted—and no longer living. When you look up to acknowledge their stern instructions to put your feet down, you will quickly notice the employee is nowhere to be found. This fanatical lifeless employee who monitors the aisles of this fine establishment has a keen way of making his presence known through sound and touch but without patrons ever seeing him.

Just like this cloaked employee, the Palace Theatre has a noteworthy reputation as a legend that refuses to resign, no matter how extraordinary the odds. The Palace Theatre has been an icon for Seguin, Texas, since the late 1930s. Besides its status as an extremely enduring cinema even against unbelievable odds, it is also recognized for the unusual spirits that linger within this grand theater's walls. Though there is no concrete reasoning for these paranormal appearances, whatever the root of these spirits' presences, they are as real as the theater's incredible survival. Although the theater has gone through some rough times, no actual deaths have been recorded on the property. Yet there are several spirits that have decided to make this durable Seguin landmark their home. To better understand *who*, it is important to recognize the possible *whys*. Understanding the building's history is the first step.

The heritage of this amazing theater actually began in 1890 with the birth of a remarkable entrepreneur named Hollis Alvin Leonard Ward "Windy" Daniel (who later added an "s" to his name to become Daniels). Daniels would grow up discovering he had a desire to explore numerous avenues when it came to jobs. Although notorious for his quick and raging temper, he was also known for being a hard worker with a warm heart who was deeply generous. He worked at a sawmill, sold newspapers, was a tailor and was even a jeweler at one time. For Daniels, though, working at a picture show in Houston taking tickets was the most captivating job of all. He was quickly hooked by the fascinating world of vaudeville and films. Daniels became a salesman for the film companies and then moved up to managing several theaters. Shortly afterward, Daniels bought numerous theaters across Texas. He owned the Guild and Alameda Theatres in Crystal City, the Teatro Azteca Theatre in Eagle Pass and the classic Dixie Drive-In of Seguin. Daniels also purchased Seguin's distinguished Texas Theatre (now known as the Stephen and Mary Birch Texas Theatre), located at 425 North Austin Street, from Alvin P. Mueller in the early 1930s. The Daniels family owned the dazzling Texas Theatre for over sixty years. They sold it in 1997 for a small sum to the Conservation Society to ensure that the theater would be preserved as a special Seguin landmark for the community to enjoy. Though Daniels also delved into the oil-well business and even a gambling place called the Spider

House, which sat on the Guadalupe River down toward the end of Reiley Road, the movie industry was his greatest joy. These were exciting times for Daniels, for he was meeting famous actors and businessmen. He was even asked by Mary Pickford and her husband, Douglass Fairbanks, to come work for them in Hollywood at their Universal Pictures, but he declined. With film production booming, Daniels then decided to solely invest in what is now called the Palace Theatre.

Though another theater had been located on the Palace's original spot sometime around 1927, according to the Sanborn Maps, as late as 1891, the land was owned by the Starcke family and had been just an empty lot. Once the theater building had been erected, it was rebuilt and renovated several times. It had been run by Daniels and two other men for a company known as the Interstate Theatres. Daniels, feeling comfortable with his knowledge and experience, eventually bought out the others around 1935 to run the Palace Theatre single-handedly and formed Seguin Theatres, Inc. He turned the Palace into the one of the finest theaters around, and it could seat up to 950 people. Its highly anticipated debut took place on May 5, 1938, with a packed house. For years, it was one of the best places to escape your

Front: "Recreation Buidling, Max Starcke Park, Seguin, Texas. 9a67-N." *Back*: "Seguin was founded in 1838, and was named in honor Col. Juan N. Seguin, a patriot of the battle of San Jaxinto. Its principal industries are pecans, cotton, oil, flour, dairy productions, and hydro-electric power generation. It is noted for its parks and municipally owned utilities. Genuine Curteich-Chicago C.T. American Art: Postcard (Reg. U.S. Pat. Off.)" *Author's private postcard collections.*

The Palace Theatre on the morning after an explosion due to a gas leak. Note the marquee in front of the building still standing. *Copyright by the Leon Studio Collection of the Heritage Museum.*

troubles and laugh away your worries. Everything was going wonderful for the Palace for many years—until one day, the once thriving theater business literally blew up.

On March 23, 1946, in the middle of the night, the city of Seguin was awakened by a sound that some locals still remember to this day. About 2:00 a.m., the ground began to rumble, shake and roar, much like the sound of an underground train. Many described feeling like an earthquake was headed their way. Soon a massive explosion could be heard by all of the citizens. They ran outside to see what had happened, and to their amazement and disbelief, the entire back portion of the Palace Theatre had been destroyed. The massive eruption had been caused by a gas leak, which tossed bricks, glass, theater chairs and other debris for blocks. Thankfully, the building was unoccupied at the time, and no one was hurt. The only original portion of the building that was left standing was one wall on the north side.

The town was horrified by this incredible accident but not natural-born entrepreneur Daniels. It simply made him go into action, setting up a large tent and folding chairs in the parking lot across the street, where he ran movies every day until the theater was rebuilt, improved and reopened in January 1947. To the citizens of Seguin, Daniels had earned his place as a respected, savvy businessman. The newly rebuilt Palace Theatre had state-

The Palace Theatre being observed by locals grateful no one had been inside at the time of the explosion. *Copyright by the Leon Studio Collection of the Heritage Museum.*

of-the-art devices for the hearing impaired, a children's crying room and a smoke room for its customers. With this newfound modern look, it also brought in movie stars on promotional tours, such as Gene Autry, Keenan Wynn, Chill Wills and even John Wayne, who in time actually became a dear friend to Daniels.

With all of the excitement of the reopening, it took a few months before locals began to notice odd things happening within this new theater. With all of its new upgrades and modern décor, of course it seemed somewhat different. Residents loved the new look and the numerous celebrities in attendance, yet people started to notice the theater's personality wasn't quite exactly the same as it used to be. Strange happenings were spoken of in soft whispers. Some thought the happenings were part of a movie promotion or commercial prank, which was common during that time. The most openly discussed incidence was the abrasive projectionist who would walk the aisles, whacking people's feet as they were resting on the seats in front of them in the darkness of the movie. However, when the customers complained, they were told the real projectionist never leaves his quarters during the film and would never hit anyone.

Even though no one was killed or even hurt during the immense destruction of the building, after the grand opening, an apparition of a finely dressed little girl, as though ready for church, would often appear on the steps leading to the second floor. She would sweetly greet guests as they walked up the stairs. When the visitors turned around, she disappeared. Then there was the forlorn young African American man dressed in tattered clothing who never spoke a word. He began to appear in the balcony with a bluish hue around him. Just by looking at him, one could tell how depressed and lost he was. Now and then, an elegant woman dressed for high tea would present herself in the ladies' bathroom downstairs as she freshened up her lipstick and checked the seams of her hosiery.

So who are these spirits, and why did they show up after the explosion? Most believe that when there is substantial change in a building, such as the explosion and renovation, spirits are awakened. The tale of the little girl states that she fell off the balcony and died. Although there have been no records found to verify this, it still could be possible. In the opinion of this author and the Ripcrew team, it is thought this spirit merely decided to spend the rest of time in a place where she had lots of wonderful memories. The sad young man is believed to have been wrongfully hanged across the street in the hanging tree in front of the Plaza Hotel since evidence from

Front: "Plaza Hotel, Seguin, Texas. 71982-N." *Back:* "My Dear Ann: This is the part of Texas I am in at the present time and it is still hot. I went to Huntington this afternoon and found a lot more hot—Ha! We have moved into a beautiful home on a small ranch out of Houston and I am sure you would like to be here. We have about 15 horses to ride anytime we want to but I can't cause I have no Cowboy boots, aint that sad. Love to all of you. Kelly." Addressed to: Miss. Ann Coyle Curry Kingsbury Place Saint Louis (13) Mo. Stamp reads Houston and San Antonio I R. 8 SFP IO 1947. 1 cent postage. *Author's private postcard collections.*

electronic voice phenomena (EVP) seemed to lead in that direction. The words "innocent" and "hung" were often spoken over numerous sessions. Of course, the hitting projectionist must have been the original Palace's employee who was saddened to see his theater demolished. As for the classy lady checking her appearance, who knows? Maybe this is where she met her soul mate on their first date or her lover on secret rendezvous or where she discovered she wanted to become an actress. In any case, all four are content to remain within the walls of the Palace Theatre.

In 1973, Windy Daniels passed away but not before proudly handing the theater business torch over to his son, H.A. "Dan" Daniels in 1967. Dan is unafraid of the spirits that linger within the building and actually accepts them as part of the history. He is exceptionally open-minded to the possibilities that ghosts may exist and is profoundly respected by paranormal enthusiasts for his openness to their continued research.

Since the larger, more modern theaters have arrived in Seguin, the Palace Theatre has changed its direction. Instead of showing the latest films, it has now wrapped its walls around the arts and hosts a variety of theatrical events, musical programs, wrestling, concerts and even paranormal investigations for the general public. What is so astonishing is that there is a third generation of the Daniels family, H.A. "Reid," learning about the theater business. With such an amazing entrepreneurial bloodline that began with "Windy" Daniels, one cannot wait to see what is in the future for the Palace Theatre with this next generation.

Chapter 2

SONKA HOUSE

TWO BUSINESSMEN BONDED BY RESPECT

The Sonka House blog (dated March 23, 2012) read: "Goodbye to Joseph Sonka? Supposedly the Sonka House will have new owners. How will they wear the mantle of nobility which is the legacy of Joseph Sonka? What if they are simple American white bourgeoisie [middle-class people] and do not know anything of the nobility of older days? This is not a house one calls one's own. This is a cornerstone of a community, history and dedication to craft."

This was the last comment left by the previous owner, Sylvia Manning, before selling the home to the next owner, Paul Hansen. It is obvious she felt somewhat attached to this building, which had been constructed by Joseph Sonka, for she even states, "Ah, I am an aging woman without maintenance skills or capitalist savvy. I was hoodwinked, I think. I feel it may be my ethical duty to stay, not leave. Oh, if I did not have other responsibilities, other duties, other promises. (By the way, as I was writing the above, all kinds of loud sounds reverberated, upstairs and down: doors slamming, things falling. I'm not particularly drawn to belief in ghost, but I think maybe…)"

This is a similar account of how the newest owner of the Sonka House, Hansen (who has transformed this remarkable building into a stunning bed-and-breakfast), described the building when being interviewed before the scheduled paranormal investigation. Hansen gave his description of the house as having a "majestic, stately character. It almost has a personality of its own." Hansen gave great praise to the original builder, Joseph Sonka, as he presented a tour of the building to the team. One could sense his admiration and deep respect for Sonka, whom he considered to be an extraordinary businessperson. Although Hansen focused mainly on the spectacular architect and history of the building as the paranormal team journeyed throughout the house, he occasionally hinted at the possibility of a spirit being present. Being somewhat of a skeptic, Hansen hesitantly claimed that at times there was an unexplainable sense of an unknown presence throughout the building and grounds. He acknowledged that it was never a threatening sensation, just a simple feeling of having someone watching over your shoulder. This building, located at 617 North Guadalupe Street, has an interesting history that is unsurpassed by many when it comes to the structure's builder, Joseph Sonka. Yet it doesn't have any substantial reason for this unusual sense of being observed, as described by Hansen. Having a decent understanding of the architect now, it was time for the paranormal team to become familiar with the home's original builder in hopes of maybe discovering a reason for this silent watcher.

Sonka was a Czechoslovakian immigrant born on April 7, 1849, who came to America in 1868. He first headed to New Braunfels but found the type of soil he needed for his bricks in Seguin. A stonemason by trade, this was the perfect location for him. He quickly purchased eleven acres of prime land and established his own brickyard. Sonka then built a cotton gin in front of the brickyard, the high smokestacks of which were the town's landmark for years. His next venture was the purchase of three additional acres of land on which to build the Sonka House. Originally, there was already a small house on the property that Sonka used while building the large house. He later incorporated that building into the big house as a servants' quarters. In 1881, construction of the Sonka House began, and it was actually to be a home for his sister. When she married, she instead moved to San Antonio, so Sonka kept the house for himself. It was completed in 1893, the same year he married Annie Klicka, whom he met at the Chicago World's Fair.

The large, two-story Sonka brick home had five bedrooms, a bath and a large hall upstairs. Downstairs, there were another five bedrooms, a bath and a large reception hall. There were three lovely fireplaces, a hand-turned staircase and beautiful hard pine floors. It had twelve-foot ceilings, and the inside walls were of thick plaster, making the walls nearly a foot deep. With the nine-foot windows and cross ventilation, air conditioning was not needed back then. One of the most interesting designs of the house is the huge basement that could be entered from either outside the building or inside. The property also contained a large carriage house. Sonka did all of the

Front: "Cotton compress, Seguin, Texas." *Back*: "Natr. Coloryte." *Author's private postcard collections.*

work himself, except for the woodwork and the stairway, which is why it took nearly twelve years to finish.

This grand home had its own water system, windmill and wells. There was a Grecian-style swimming pool to the north of the house in his plans. To the south of the pool, there was a pavilion with a stage where dances were often held. The property included a skating rink, a basketball court and even a bowling alley, built sometime between 1902 and 1906. Just north of the big house, Sonka constructed a two-story building that housed a grocery store and saloon on the bottom and a meeting place for the Hermann Sons Lodge on the second floor. At this same location, Sonka added a three-bedroom apartment in the rear to serve as his family's temporary residence while their large home was donated to serve as a community hospital, called the Seguin Sanitarium, from 1913 to 1915. It was an incredible offer to make to his community.

Sonka also built a long single-story home with a large porch and fireplaces in every room beside his big house and gave it to his mother and father. Sonka seemed to be able to handle adversity as well as prosperity, for when fire destroyed his gin in 1899, it wasn't long before he rebuilt and was once again hard at work. In 1902, tragedy struck when Sonka lost his arm in an unfortunate accident at the gin. He fell into the jaws of the cotton gin and was badly cut in the side and face. His right arm was so badly mangled that

The Sonka House after being turned into Seguin Sanitarium. Note the sign on the building. *Copyright by the Leon Studio Collection of the Heritage Museum.*

it had to be amputated. This slowed him down for a while, but he kept on with his many ingenious plans.

The house was full of fun and love as his four children grew into adulthood. One child after another finished school and either went off for more schooling or off to work. But their happiness was shattered on April 5, 1924, when Joseph Sonka died at the age of seventy-five. Even though some of the children came home on weekends, the old house just wasn't the same. It was way too quiet for Sonka's widow, Mrs. Annie Klicka Sonka. Thinking creatively like her husband, she then decided to divide the large house into apartments for rent. From then on, she always had someone in her house and was never alone.

By 1929, oil had been discovered in Darst Creek, just on the eastern outskirts of Seguin, and everyone was renting rooms. There were few vacant rooms to be had, so Mrs. Sonka could take her choice of how many boarders she wanted to rent to. Then, in 1930, Randolph Field opened, and another influx of renters came. Mrs. Sonka was never without lots of people in her home. The old house was happy again until Mrs. Sonka passed away on May 31, 1937. Now it was left for their daughters, Irene, Lillian and Mayme, who at one time or another all moved back into the house and accepted the duties of renting out the rooms. The building was then lovingly nicknamed the "Sisters Home." The only Sonka son, Mylos, lived in San Antonio until he passed away in 1952. The sisters continued to rent rooms and apartments until 1975, when they decided they no longer wanted to bother with all it required. They just wanted to retire and take it easy. The house was sold and changed hands a few times until it was fortunate to be purchased by its current owner, Paul Hansen.

As you listen to Hansen, one can easily sense his dedication and commitment to this building. He has now divided the building into two separate sections, with one section being the bed-and-breakfast, with four rooms for guests, and the other being the separate living quarters for the owner. Hansen's zest for the future of this bed-and-breakfast is breathtaking. As he explained each upcoming renovation, his eyes lit up with anticipation. The landscaping is exquisite, as is the interior decorating. What are most exciting are his plans to serve full-course meals, which is rare in the bed-and-breakfast realm. There is even talk of a wine room in the cellar. When he speaks of the building's prospects, it is exhilarating to listen. Hansen definitely has an entrepreneur's way of thinking and a huge respect for the building.

As the team learned more about the building's first owner, Sonka, and its present one, Hansen, it all began to make sense. After completing the paranormal investigation, the only tangible evidence captured were movements of faint shadow figures, knocking or hammering on the walls and that overwhelming sense of being watched. Was the feeling of being monitored and scrutinized in this house a coincidence? Not hardly. Sonka was a man who had a dream, forged ahead and never gave up. Even his wife and daughters maintained that same way of thinking when it came to this building. Paul Hansen has the same personality. This is the common denominator for the connection between these two owners. Sonka and Hansen have similar "never give up" personalities and a mutual understanding of being dedicated entrepreneurs. Both men have determination and perseverance when it comes to their passion for business and this building. The unanimous decision reached by the paranormal team was easy. This building is not as haunted as one would think, having been a sanitarium at one time. Instead, it pays homage to a remarkable man who is still monitoring his building's future. The feeling of being watched over your shoulder is merely Joseph Sonka keeping an eye on his home. It is believed Sonka probably has great admiration and trust for Hansen since he is so diligent in the building's improvements. Nonetheless, one can bet Joseph Sonka is still watching and monitoring the progress of his most prized possession.

Chapter 3

THE AUMONT HOTEL

THE RESCUE BY A REVEREND

When beginning the investigation of the Aumont Hotel, located at 301 North Austin Street, there was a lot of speculation about why this building was considered to be haunted. There were tales of the insane dead tenant who tries to trip you as you begin your flight up the stairs and the slithering presence that wraps itself around your legs as you walk into the basement. With all these frightful descriptions, the team decided to invite its dear friend Reverend Mark to attend the event just in case. Funny though, until you do your homework, it truly is just that: speculation. Now having been present at this profound investigation, this haunting was far from what was had been described by the public. It actually was just the opposite. This investigation became one of the greatest spiritual encounters experienced by those who were present and witnessed it. Strangely enough, it began with the words of a young disembodied female voice asking for a reverend.

The paranormal crew members were prepared for what they were told could possibly be an intensely frightening experience. The accounts of the hotel's hauntings were described as violent, alarming and dangerous. However, two hours into the investigation, the team learned this was far from the actual truth.

During the first EVP session, the initial sound was a voice heard over the digital recorder saying, "Howdy" as the investigators walked in the entrance. The presence of something kind engulfed the lobby. The team described it as a feeling of "hanging out with the boys." The team laughed and said, "Well, this isn't very menacing! Cool, but not threatening, thank goodness." Then they headed to the gorgeous ballroom, which has an alluring way about it that makes you want to spring into a waltz. As they set up the night-vision cameras, shadow figures were strongly evident right away. Everyone agreed this was simply the residual effect of the elegant parties that were once held in this delightful room. Then the team headed to the basement. This decision would cause several of the paranormal team members to rethink how they feel about existing spirits and the afterlife. It was to be a lovely and touching development that those present will never forget.

The team members had known about the hotel's history but nothing about what was about to confront them. The team knew that the Aumont's architect had been the well-known Atlee B. Ayres, and it opened in November 1916. The Aumont had been part of what Seguin called the "Hotel Wars" with the 1917 Park Hotel (later named the Plaza) built by M.J. Dielman. It began when the shrewd businessmen of Seguin made the decision that they needed a new hotel since the city's first hotel, the Magnolia, had lost some of its gorgeous antebellum luster after seventy-five years. Plus, times were financially good for Seguin in 1916. On top of that, a recent fire had destroyed an entire block of buildings downtown, and local Seguin citizens were eager to rebuild. The city announced that the Aumont was about to be built, and then no more than three weeks later, it was announced there would be another new hotel constructed. Where this rivalry originated between these two hotels is still unknown, but it has been suggested that the two groups were divided on lines of political loyalty or simply on what side of the town they happened to live, north or south of Court Street. The people watched as the competing buildings went up. Details and gossip about the buildings were hilariously rampant. The phone company installed a total of eighty-two telephones in both hotels on the exact same day so that there would be no signs of favoritism toward either side. Ridiculously, the number of hotel rooms for a city the size of Seguin was twenty-two rooms per one thousand people, which was an even higher average than New York City. With the overabundance of rooms, the Park (Plaza) eventually was transformed into a sanatorium in 1927 for three years and then returned to a hotel, but in the end, it was put up for sale. The Aumont eventually became apartments, and its present owner is Keith Giles. It is also rented out for meetings, social events and even movie sets. When the paranormal team members were completely informed of the building's background, they headed into the supposedly eerie basement.

Front: "Aumont Hotel, Seguin, Texas." *Back*: "C.T. doubletone. Ad-12919." I love the old lampposts along the street. *Author's private postcard collections.*

As they sat there for a while, allowing the room to calm and show its personality, the entire team agreed there was nothing bad existing. If anything, the room was filled with a sense of gratefulness for their presence. No sooner had they sat down for a long night of EVP sessions than the K2 meters lit up, and the ghost box (a scanning radio receiver that picks up white noise allowing spirits to create words, even sentences) began an incredible conversation with the team that would leave its members emotionally drained. The spirit box quickly said "chaplain," then "help," "the light" and "wanting to leave." Thankfully, having invited Reverend Mark to the event, he was summoned to join them. What was to follow seemed nothing less than jaw-dropping to those who watched. The area was energized by the spirits' strong presence, the lengthy detailed conversation at hand and the team's psychic, who was overwhelmed by the emotion of everyone in the room. When the reverend entered the room, he said, "Oh my, this is very real, isn't it, guys?" Reverend Mark said he could feel the sensation of cheerfulness as he entered the room. The team explained that the ghost had revealed certain phrases through the spirit box, hinting at its possible wishes, and had even requested a "chaplain." The reverend's response was so beautiful. He said, "This is a gentle spirit who is ready to go to the light and is grateful we are here to help." Then the reverend said the Last Rites and Dedication of the Soul as the whole team prayed. Next, he spoke to the spirit in a "one-on-one" type of conversation, explaining to this spirit that she had made the right decision to move on. It was beautiful beyond words. The last words on the EVP recorder were "Thank you." Then the reverend said, "She's with God now." There wasn't a dry eye in the building. What was even more amazing was that this session was being Skyped for the team's followers and fans to watch the investigation live, and even the audience was weighing in with their emotions.

It was hard for the team to continue with the investigation after this powerful episode. Such endings are rare in the paranormal investigative realm. Teams desperately want to learn about spirits while doing their research, but assisting a spirit in finding help is the crown jewel. It is the ultimate goal for a paranormal researcher. That night, the team members experienced it firsthand, and it changed them forever. They will probably never know who the trusting spirit was, but for them, it didn't matter. All they knew was that it had asked them for their help, and mercifully, they had a reverend on hand. The Aumont is still active with other spirits that linger within the building. Though it is a building full of cheerful and contented ghosts—especially the cowboy, who quickly greets you with a "Howdy" at the door, and the waltzing dancers in the ballroom—none will ever top the spirit that made its way to where it wanted to be with the help of the Ripcrew team and Reverend Mark.

Chapter 4

THE MAGNOLIA HOTEL

A SECRET REVEALED

When he entered the Voeckler home, it was his intention to kill only his wife, but the young Emma awoke, and there couldn't be any witnesses. Emil Voeckler walked in before Faust could finish murdering his wife. After the attack, Faust threw the axe in the Guadalupe River, burned his bloody clothes and changed into new clothes. He then rode the stolen horse hard back to the Magnolia Hotel as quickly as possible, arriving around 5:00 a.m.

The above is a small snippet from my book *Haunted New Braunfels*. Although the story was merely three pages long in the manuscript, it would drastically end up changing my course, as well as that of my family and those who were drawn in by the lure of an unwavering young female ghost with a secret she desperately wanted to tell the world. This amazingly strong child spirit had a determined goal to accomplish and was relentless. This would be the first spirit I have come across that truly and persistently sought the guidance of a living person and achieved her mission. She is to be admired by all those who discover her story.

After writing the chapter "The Voeckler Murder: The Comaltown Ghost" about a young girl named Emma brutally murdered in her bed, I became consumed with the need to know more about this case. It was important to know Emma's family history and—even odder—the background of her murderer and his family's past. Though the book's manuscript was completed and even published, I became preoccupied with knowing more about all those involved in the Voecklers' murder case. I often dreamt about this little girl twirling at her dance class, which was her last pleasant moment experienced before dying. In my dreams, she was always reaching her hand out to me as if she wanted to take me someplace. At one point, it actually became an obsession to at least locate the building once known as the Magnolia Hotel. It was somehow important to stand in the room occupied by this senseless killer who could just calmly sleep the night away after committing the horrendous murder of an innocent child. This was way out of the norm for me. Staying away from negative energy is my strongest goal in life, for it serves no purpose. After awhile, the fixation to discover the hotel's location seemed more than sheer curiosity; it felt like a calling. There was definitely something beyond my control taking the reins on this unusual journey.

The search for this elusive building began unexpectedly when I turned to my older sister, Mickey, who has lived in Seguin for years, to ask if she had ever heard of a Magnolia Hotel. Before I could even utter the words, she handed me an old newspaper article. When I looked down, it was a clipping of a story about a building in danger of being torn down. To my surprise, it was none other than the Magnolia Hotel. I gasped and asked her how she knew I was looking for this building. She seemed so confused by my reaction. She stated since I was a historian she simply thought it would be an interesting read. Coincidence? No way. There is no such thing as coincidence, in my opinion. I knew something paranormally amazing was happening, so I raced to my computer. Sparks flew from the keyboard as I entered the name Magnolia Hotel in the search engine. It then guided me to a recently released video on YouTube created by Seguin Main Street

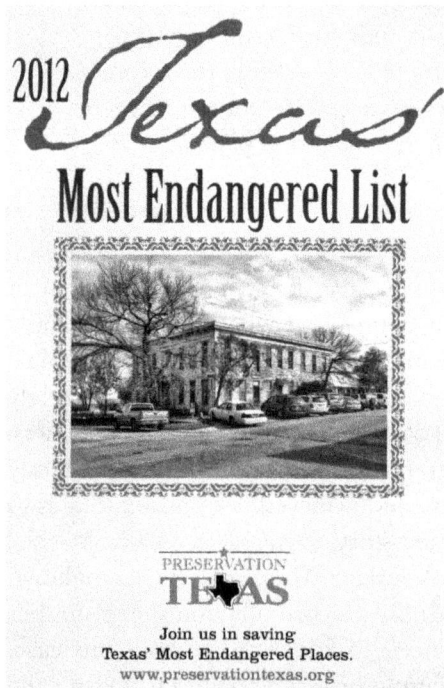

Courtesy of Preservation Texas.

Program director Mary Jo trying to save a building called the Magnolia Hotel that was listed on the 2013 Texas Most Endangered Places.

One could certainly tell this building was special and meant a great deal to local historians, which was intriguing. How could they cherish a building that once played such a huge part in a murderer's life? As I scrolled down the computer screen, there was a comment that said, "Video sponsored by Realtor Bill Bender with Bender Realty, LLC in Seguin." Thus began the journey. With a contact name in hand—and a realtor, at that—with any luck, maybe now it would be possible to simply see inside. The realtor was contacted in the hopes that I might be given a tour of this building up for sale—or so I thought. Surprisingly, the agent, Bender, said the building was not on the market. Just when I thought there was no chance of entering the building, he went on to say, "But I do know the owner well. Let me see what I can do." Although my husband and I were actually seeking a small building to restore at this exact time, I never stated I was interested in purchasing the hotel. This building was way too big of a project for us to take on, yet oddly, the realtor assumed without questioning that we were very serious buyers. It was as if he knew we were to be the buyers even before we did.

Strangely enough, after that phone call, the domino effect began. From then on, everything fell into place. It was as if a stronger force were manning the controls. Though we were still seeking only to look at the building, the hotel obviously had other plans for us. One of the three owners, Laura, met with Bender and agreed to at least show the building but with no guarantees it would be available for purchase. This was fine with us, for we still were merely wishing to see inside and had not even considered purchasing it. The building's needs were way too large for our undertaking, so we had a closed mind about buying it. All we wanted to do was look inside, take a few pictures and move on. The day of walking through those doors could not come fast enough. Just knowing we were about to enter this grand old hidden building was exciting, but we had no idea this brief visit was going to end up changing our lives forever.

As the petite, charismatic co-owner Laura walked toward us, we liked her right away. She was extremely captivating from the start of the conversation. Her kindness, energy and love for the building was contagious. Before beginning the walkthrough of the entire building, the first question we asked was, "Is the building haunted?" She politely giggled and swiftly said, "No way. I lived here all my life, and it is not haunted." She fondly spoke only of the building's enormous history and wonderful memories of her family

The Magnolia Hotel around 1920. *Copyright by the Leon Studio Collection of the Heritage Museum.*

living on the bottom floor. Laura stated how the front two bottom rooms were the original log house with a breezeway in the middle built in 1840 by one of Seguin's co-founders, James Campbell. The cabin and land were then sold in 1844 to Joseph F. Johnson, who then turned it into Seguin's first stagecoach station and added the limecrete building in the back. Even the authentic bell that once belonged to the actual famous Alamo hung in the front yard of the hotel for years until it was rightfully returned to the mission. The location of the bell, a rock stump that has still endured over the years, had earned its spot in history. It was used as a footstep for the slave children to ring the famous bell announcing the arrival of the stagecoach passengers. We hadn't even walked inside yet, and our mouths were already dropping in awe of the history of the building. Laura affectionately explained what it was like to live on the entire bottom floor of the building during her childhood with her grandparents (who purchased the building in 1930) Edgar and Inez Lannom. After the Lannoms bought the building, they had renovated the bottom floor into their residence, and the top floor became apartments designed mainly for the Darst oilmen.

Then as Laura turned the key to the lock attached to a dilapidated, old door with its paint peeling off, the most extraordinary thing happened.

"Historic American Buildings Survey, Arthur W. Stewart, Photographer April 29, 1936 WEST ELEVATION (SIDE). Magnolia Hotel, 203 South Crockett Street, Seguin, Guadalupe County, TX." *Library of Congress, Prints & Photographs Division, HABS HABS TEX,94-SEGUI,2—3.*

"Historic American Buildings Survey, Arthur W. Stewart, Photographer April 29, 1936 NORTH ELEVATION (FRONT). Magnolia Hotel, 203 South Crockett Street, Seguin, Guadalupe County, TX." *Library of Congress, Prints & Photographs Division, HABS HABS TEX,94-SEGUI,2—1.*

"Historic American Buildings Survey, Arthur W. Stewart, Photographer April 29, 1936 NORTHEAST EEVATION (NORTH FRONT AND EAST SIDE). Magnolia Hotel, 203 South Crockett Street, Seguin, Guadalupe County, TX." *Library of Congress, Prints & Photographs Division, HABS.[HABS TEX,94-SEGUI,2—2.*

Although she continued to speak, we were completely unaware of her words. As she gradually opened the entrance to the hotel, my husband, Jim, and I could unmistakably feel the building reach out and grab hold of us. It was as though the building were greeting us with open arms. All we could do was look at each other, knowing something special was happening. If the building could speak, the sounds of happy sighing and welcome would have been heard. We were completely and utterly spellbound.

As we slowly entered the building on the bottom floor, we noticed how it had the most pleasant atmosphere about it. Even though it was completely jampacked with old furniture and miscellaneous items, making it hard to move around freely, it looked like a palace to us. One could easily sense there had been numerous good times, happy guest and friendly visitors since the mid-1800s. Each room felt as though a friendly get-together had just ended, especially in what is called the children's room. It was a delightful feeling that was hard to walk away from. As we moved from room to room, there was a sense of pleasant spirits all around us as if they were giving the tour.

Then the door leading upstairs was opened, and it was a completely different feeling. Even Jim, who was a skeptic then, took a step back at first.

Just as soon as we began walking up the steps leading to the second floor, the sensation of the building drastically changed. It was an odd feeling, as though the air was heavy, making it hard to breathe. The best way to explain it was that it felt like entering an extremely crowded and overpacked floor of people. The energy of numerous spirits engulfed the entire floor, though this was not surprising. Since the building had been a hotel and then apartments for over one hundred years, the residual feeling of the residents' presences would definitely be understandable. Yet this floor had more than just that. There were without a doubt strong individual presences among us. The transformation between the atmospheres of the two floors was like night and day. Each room upstairs had a completely different character to it, however. It was intensely bizarre sensing so many unusual feelings throughout the top floor. One apartment would be filled with sadness and heaviness, and then the next had a giddy feeling, as if a child were present. Strangely, the worst sensation came from the pink bathroom. Jim and I thought it was just the hideous paint coloring causing the creepy feeling. Then, as we proceeded throughout the labyrinth-like architecture of the building, we turned the corner, guided by the owner, and there it was: Room #3. This was the room of William Faust, who, after murdering a young girl and blinding his wife, simply curled up in this small bedroom to sleep the night away. It was strange, though, that after striving for so long to stand in the middle of this room to get a sense of how evil this man could be, the feeling was just the opposite. Indeed, the room was full of hostility, hatred and an overall distaste for our presence, which was no surprise. But there was also an overwhelming sense of intense fear, as though standing next to a coward frightened by our company. Strange, as this was not expected of such a ruthless, cruel killer. What could this possibly mean? Why would this brutal murderer have fear toward us? What was even stranger was that the current owner had no idea this building had once lodged a brutal murderer on the top floor. How could this fact remain unknown for her entire life up until that point? One thing was for certain: we had no apprehensions about being in that room. If William Faust was truly present, there was nothing to be afraid of. It was he who was more fearful of us. What was even more confusing was that there were more intense menacing moods throughout the rest of the top floor, leaving Faust's room to feel the least threatening. This left me confused and wondering what it was that Emma was trying to get me to know.

Although trying to absorb the owner's profound words, all that we could focus on was the captivating allure of this building. Despite the fact that the top floor had an unusual feeling to it, the building itself was enormously historic and desperately needed rescuing. Plus, the building had such a hold on us that it was hard to walk away. Even though we were actually in the market for a historic building to do minor restorations as a weekend project, we never expected we would consider purchasing such a massive structure in need of huge repairs. Nevertheless, from the moment the tour began, we knew the building was to be ours. For weeks, all that was on our minds was this unbelievable hotel. It felt as though the building would not allow us to forget it. Now we had the task at hand of convincing three siblings to sell their childhood home, and we made an offer to buy it. Although the building had fallen into disrepair over the years, this was still their childhood home and hard for them to let go of. It took several months of negotiating, but with the grace of God, the trust of the three siblings and the help of a great realtor in March 2013, the Magnolia Hotel's future was handed over to us. From that day forward, Jim's life and mine have not been the same, yet we would not change it for the world.

The same day we signed the papers, we headed over to the hotel to allow the previous owners to remove their last few personal items remaining but mainly to allow them to say goodbye to it. As they finished loading their private mementos from the bottom two rooms in front, we also gave a few of our own family members a brief tour. After everyone left, Jim and I headed into the one-story white limecrete building to take a look-see. This three-room building was, in fact, the original Magnolia Hotel built in 1844 by Joseph F. Johnson, who owned the stagecoach station. It was also where the legendary Texas Ranger captain John "Jack" Coffee Hays married Susan Calvert in front of the charming fireplace with a sign that reads, "Home Sweet Home" embedded over the mantle. After the two-story hotel was built between the stagecoach station and the adobe building by Dr. Read and Carpenter in 1850, this three-room structure became the servants' quarters. Of the entire building, this section was in the best condition. The last owners of the hotel were the Lannoms, and when they passed, they willed the building to Laura and her brothers. The two-story hotel had fallen into great disrepair, but the servants' quarters had been kept up nicely. Because of this, they had been renting it out as an apartment for years. As it was the cleanest and most well-kept area of the building, we decided to toast our good fortune of newly owning the hotel in this location. As we popped open our champagne, filled our glasses and raised them for a toast, we soon discovered the owner, Laura, was quite mistaken about the house not being haunted. Just as we were about to clink our glasses in salute, we encountered our very first spirit.

As we raised our glasses, there was a sudden burst of cold air that went directly between us both, and the blocked opened door slammed shut and the lights began to flicker. We both knew we were not alone in the room but were completely unafraid. It was not a bad impression. This encounter seemed more like a spirit wishing only to make its presence known. Without a doubt, it did just that—in fact, it made a grand entrance and has never left.

Every time we returned to the hotel, these types of paranormal events became more numerous. Not one day would go by without something unusual occurring in the building. Strange things happening during the restoration quickly became normal episodes. Cabinet doors would continuously open and close, shadow figures were seen and the sound of furniture being moved on the second floor could be heard though all of the rooms were empty. Footsteps, laughter, humming and knocking were often audible. The most profound experience was hearing our own names called out by a female voice when no one else was in the building. Gentle tugging at our clothes and pulling of our hair were becoming commonplace physical encounters. Then, as pictures of the building and individual rooms were being taken for insurance purposes, peculiar images began to appear. There was the snapshot of playful children staring and smiling into my camera and the silhouettes of two shadows on the wall of the bathroom, though I was all alone. The most powerful photos were the different faces captured looking outward through the windows from the inside when no one was in the building. Then something bizarre happened that forever altered the atmosphere of the hotel.

Loaded with cleaning solutions, a mop and a broom one day, I plopped them down on the table. As Jim began his favorite task of pulling the high weeds in the yard, I went back out to my car and brought in dowsing rods for a simple experiment after I tidied up the servants' quarters. Having heard that the dowsing rods were instruments occasionally used by paranormal teams and that they required no skills, I thought it couldn't hurt to attempt to get to the bottom of these uncanny experiences. Strangely enough, as soon as the rods were brought into the adobe building, the energy of the room quickly changed. The devices began to have warmth to them, even a slight tingle to the touch. My arms began to have a prickling feeling, and then a sense of contentment filled the room. It was startling at first, yet beautiful at the same time. There was a strong presence standing in my pathway, and it was obvious something was making its existence known. Stunned by this overwhelming sudden episode, I dropped the rods to the floor. Though not frightened, I had just never felt such a surge of energy before. I quickly called Jim in from outside, and what happened next was more extraordinary than can be properly conveyed.

I could hear a soft, calming voice in the form of a thought telling me not to be afraid and to pick up the rods again. As I nervously reached and then picked them up, the room was swiftly charged once again with energy. This time, there wasn't just one spirit present; there were multiple. Although most people would probably get up and run in fear for their lives, there was no threatening feeling at all. In fact, it was quite pleasant, as though being among a group of friends. With the rods tightly clutched in my hands, the first session of communication began between me and this very determined spirit as Jim looked on.

For months on end, there were question-and-answer sessions between the spirit and myself that provided an overabundance of information. One could tell this tenacious spirit was helping other spirits to gradually come forward and reveal themselves. Though we eventually discovered who these spirits were, why they lingered within the walls of this grand old building had not yet been shared with us. They could only guide us to the destination they sought. Our task at hand was to discover why they remained earthbound and seek out others who could guide them. Thus began a quest of each individual spirit within the hotel that would leave not only myself but also others filled with mixed emotions. Several people were then called on by the silent allure of the rods' strength. It came in somewhat of a mental telepathy beckoning them to visit the building, leaving them confused, surprised and anxious to help the unknown spirits find their answers. From that day on, the Magnolia Hotel and numerous unsuspecting guests (including myself) would never be the same. The spirits within the building now had a way of communicating, and they refused to stop.

Thereafter, someone knocking on the Magnolia Hotel's door wishing to share how they were connected to the hotel became a daily ritual. At times, it was a bit overwhelming, but they felt so obligated to have their stories heard that it was hard to turn them away. Each story began with the speaker having either lived there or being related to someone once connected to the building. Descendants from James Campbell, Juan Seguin and even the building's architect, Tobias Meininger, came to visit. The history gathered from these conversations was invaluable and helped in the research immensely. Then, after all the history connections were depleted, a bizarre pattern began to unfold. Honestly, it was hard to comprehend. People began to show up at the door, stating they just felt compelled to visit and asking to come inside. They had no connection (so they thought) and explained that it was as though the building had called them. For the sake of time, individual tours were out of the question, but we offered occasional private group tours to those who seemed deeply interested. By openly speaking to the spirits and acknowledging their presence, one could sense trust among the spirits at these gatherings. It also provided comfort and eventually a clearer understanding of these unsuspecting visitors' intense need to attend. Without a doubt, they had been drawn in at the request of the spirits without them even knowing.

During one of the earlier group tours consisting of nearly twenty people, the first and most profound guest whose reason for visiting was revealed. She was a delightful, shy and somewhat skeptical woman named Tnisha. As soon as she walked in the door, the room was energized, and I knew without a doubt that she was there for a purpose. As the tour began, the building was hopping with paranormal activity, and the guests were intrigued. The ghost box, a tool used for communication, was emitting names that matched ancestors of the guests attending. After the tour, we all returned to the adobe building. As a test, I picked up the dowsing rods, and as if with a magnetic pull, they were drawn with great intensity toward Tnisha. To be honest, the strength of the dowsing rods' energy toward her even made me take a step back. After numerous questions were directed to her trying to understand what the spirit was trying to convey, it was discovered that Tnisha was a direct descendant of Seguin's famous fortuneteller, Idella Lampkin. It is widely known that Idella did many psychic readings at the Magnolia Hotel for her clients. This connection to Idella was astonishing to Tnisha because she had no idea they were related. This would be just the first of various connections to be discovered over time. It would also become the beginning of people drawn to the hotel to discover Idella was still telling fortunes and working her magic.

As more and more visitors arrived at the hotel, the dowsing rods and I seemed to merely be a channel for Idella's work and guidance. People would arrive bewildered and confused by their overwhelming desire to visit the hotel. After a brief interview with them, we would discover they were somehow connected to the building, and their personal spirit simply wanted to convey a message. Though some would enter as skeptics, they left believers. Most arrived not even knowing why they were there, but they would leave knowing their visit had a purpose. Although some visitors' reasons have not been revealed yet, just their presence brought great delight to some of the Magnolia Hotel's spirits. For example, Allison brightened the days of the tiny spirit known as Itsy, who was left alone for long periods of time. Robbie and Wiley could make the ball roll in the children's room without touching it; Dawn and Susie were among the few people who were unafraid of giving tours upstairs alone; and sweet, young Katrina's presence was enjoyed by the Magnolia Hotel's famous escort, known as Pink Rosebud. This list goes on and on. The building definitely loved the company of the visitors, and the guests enjoyed the experience. With the help of historical research, Ripcrew's paranormal research and psychics, plus the channeling help of Idella and the dowsing rods, people were discovering they had connections to the building's spirits, and answers were being revealed about why certain spirits remain.

Two such spirits include those of William and Jennie, a brother and sister who became orphans in the late 1800s. Jennie was adopted by relatives, but William was left to fend for himself at age ten. The son of the Magnolia Hotel owner, Rollin Johnston, took William in as his own. When William was old enough, he sent for his sister to come live at the hotel. The Magnolia was William and Jennie's happiest place ever. Jennie died giving birth to her second son, but William went on to marry and have eight children and embark on a career as a Seguin firefighter. It is believed that William and Jennie remain at the Magnolia, enjoying the childhood they never had.

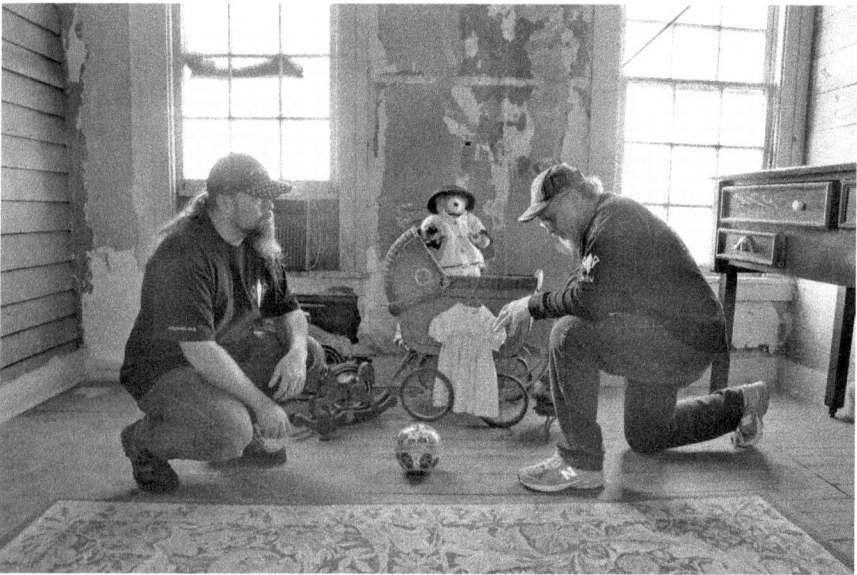

Ripcrew Paranormal Team's co-founders Robbie Prince (left) and Wiley Uzzell asking the spirits in the Magnolia Hotel's children's room to roll the ball. *Photo by Megan Foster.*

The shadow figure spirit that stands by the doorway leading into the adobe area is the mentally disturbed man who tried to kill himself while riding on the stagecoach. The other passengers restrained him, but no sooner had he gotten off the carriage than he shot himself to death in front of the entrance to the original Magnolia Hotel and the guests.

Then there is the distraught woman who has been seen looking out the window of the ballroom. The tale goes that she was waiting at the stagecoach station for her sweetheart to arrive on the carriage, but sadly, he never reached his destination. They say she waited for days and days without eating, hoping he just missed his scheduled time, yet her lover was never to be seen again. It is believed she is still waiting for her beloved as she stares out the window.

Seguin's well-known escort was made famous in the book *True Women*, written by Janice Woods Windle. *Copyright by the Leon Studio Collection of the Heritage Museum.*

In the smoke room, there is a shadow figure that has been seen day and night. This is believed to be James Campbell, the original owner of the two-room log house. He was preparing for a trip to San Antonio with a group of men he had hired for his protection. Raiding Indians were rampant at the time. Sadly, even with extra men by his side, he still met an untimely death. When he woke up the next morning to begin his journey, his horse had wandered away, or so he thought. When he went looking for it, he was jumped by a party of Indians. He was killed, scalped and stripped of his clothes and belongings. The murdering Indians were eventually killed, and Campbell's body was retrieved and buried. It is believed this room is where Campbell spent his last day alive, and he probably wishes he hadn't gone outside. The Magnolia Hotel is his haven where he has chosen to remain.

Although the list of discovered reasons for why the spirits remain is lengthy, none can match the reason behind the most profound of all of them, sweet Emma. The journey of the discovery of this grand hotel began while searching for the final location of a murderer whose victim was a young girl. Now that path has led to the unveiling of why Emma sent Jim and me here. We completely understand now the reason for the feeling of hatred, weakness, vulnerability and cowardice in William's room. Emma, William's tiny victim, was indeed given the last laugh in William's destiny. Using her strong channeling power to draw in descendants, Idella would remarkably guide someone to unknowingly disclose an amazing secret that could possibly liberate this special child from her earthbound restrictions. After speaking at one of my book signings, a beautiful, tranquil woman came up to me and asked if she could chat a bit. I knew she was someone special because the feeling seemed almost spiritual as she looked me in the eyes. She asked if I would not disclose the location of William Faust's burial location in my book. It seems that in the past, his headstone had been vandalized several times by people who already knew of his story, and she was trying to help discourage this. She wanted to help the family avoid having to go through this unpleasantness ever again. Of course I agreed. I asked her if by chance she was related to Faust since she was concerned about the cemetery, and she grinned and answered with a polite, "No." Out of pure curiosity, I then asked why would she was be so concerned about Faust's cemetery if not related. Her answer took my breath away. She said, "Because I'm a descendant of Emma. We feel sorry for his wife's extended family, the Rhodiuses, and how it all ended."

I was flabbergasted. Her ancestor had been murdered, and she felt sorry for the murderer's wife and her family. Never have I experienced such pure compassion and forgiveness. It was mind-boggling. I asked what she meant by "how it all ended." Then she spoke the words that answered everything. I still get chills today thinking about it. The gentle lady said, "Oh, don't you know? It was Emma's father who shot William Faust to death through the courthouse window. The sheriff had moved Faust to the least protected area to allow the child's father to take vengeance in his own hands. If you think about it, the sheriff never looked for Faust's killer, and the town was OK with that. It was a hush-hush topic that no one ever spoke of after his death. The town felt justice had been served."

There it was, the reason I felt compelled to locate the Magnolia Hotel that led to this woman and her secret. Little Emma had big news she wanted everyone to know and was determined to tell the world. She had guided me to her story in New Braunfels and then led me to locate a building that held not only the spirit of her murderer but also that of a fortuneteller who can channel and attract people who could help reveal her secret. It seems it was important for her to let the world know that, in her father's eyes, justice was served. He had stated that he felt ashamed he had not been there to protect his young daughter. Emma wanted everyone to know that her father had taken things into his own hands in the end after all. William knew all along that Emma was guiding me to the truth, and this is why his room was full of shame and cowardice. Now when I walk in the room, I know why he is keeping his distance, which is OK with me.

The Magnolia Hotel is an incredibly historic building. The building was once a log home to one of Seguin's co-founders, a stagecoach station, a pre-railroad hotel, one of the last remaining limecrete structures, a wedding chapel to a famous Texas Ranger, a saloon, a fabulous diner and apartments, and it protected women and children in the Indian raid shelter when needed. This building has seen thousands of visitors walk through its door from 1840 to present. It was a place of great parties, dinners and raising children. Now it is also home to those who do not wish to leave. These spirits still have stories to tell and secrets to share, or they simply wish to remain for eternity in a place they once loved. Perhaps, like the spirit of William Faust, some are doomed to remain until our creator deems otherwise. I now am left with the question: what happens after a spirit finally exposes what they were asking of me? Will Emma leave the Magnolia Hotel now that her precious secret is revealed? One can only hope she will if this is what she wants. Jim and I just want her to be happy. She has been in my life for nearly five years at this writing, and I see her as family now. If she chooses to remain, we will love, cherish and protect her for as long as we live and have already made arrangements for the building's protection and care when we pass ourselves. Wherever she decides to go, we are grateful for having crossed her path. We have already captured an EVP of a spirit we believe is Governor Ireland, the prosecutor of William Faust, telling us of his future. Governor Ireland, whom we feel has been protecting us against William, stated in the kindest male voice, "I'm going home now." This message was both sad and happy at the same time. He, too, had completed his task, so we believe and will miss him.

As for Idella, she is still drawing people in. Her latest is another one of her own descendants known as "Q." I can't really explain why the Magnolia Hotel is such a tender portal for spirits. We do know that more and more new spirits keep revealing themselves. Some say Idella has spread the word that this is a fine place to hang your hat. No matter though; as they continue to appear, we will carry on our commitment to help them find their way. To us, this is a loving building with kind spirits only wishing to find their way home or discover their descendants. Maybe someday Idella will have her way and put on a grand family reunion at the hotel once it is finished. One thing is for sure: if anyone could pull this off, this amazing spirit could get it done. Oh, and if you ever get to visit the hotel someday, be sure to ask for a lucky button. It's an amazing story, and some say Idella is spreading her magic with these tiny trinkets.

Chapter 5

WOMAN HOLLERING CREEK

LA LLORONA

If you have ever journeyed on Texas's most traveled thoroughfare called Interstate 10, then you must have noticed the abundant road signs with unusually labeled creeks along the way. The names are rather peculiar at times, but oddly enough, most of the creek beds are dry as a bone. This can leave one to question the reasoning for the strange branding of these creeks and also to wonder why they are described as bodies of water to begin with when most of the time they are empty. To help clear this up, it's important to understand how Texas defines a creek. It is a body of water with a flow sometimes during the year that is confined within its banks, and it streams into a larger body of water, such as a lake, river or even another creek. Mostly these creeks just dissolve into the ground, but that's Texas for you. As far as the naming goes, in this great state, most creeks were named by early settlers for what they had noticed when they first arrived in the area. Some are self-explanatory and named for an animal first seen, such as Catfish, Buffalo and Fox Creeks. Then there are those that are named for the description of the creek, like Brushy, Dry and Cedar. Even Indian tribes like Caddo, Tecovas and Keechie that once settled in the area laid claim to certain creeks. Then there are events that occurred there and gave a depressingly literal suggestion for a name, such as Scalp Creek, Burnt Boot Creek and Calamity Creek. Such curious labeling allows one's mind to question the reason for such intense names. Seguin retains ownership of one of the most peculiarly named streams in Texas: the Woman Hollering Creek.

This unusually titled creek, which heads south under Interstate 10 just slightly east of San Antonio toward Seguin, is considered to be one of Texas's most highly disputed mysteries when it comes to the possible cause of its naming. Woman Hollering Creek is without a doubt an extremely well-known creek in Seguin. Yet for those who know the truth, they realize its notoriety is not solely for its strange labeling. This creek is far more known for the bizarre, gloomy occurrences that can be heard and sometimes seen in the early hours of the morning.

For years, people have wondered and speculated on the reason for this waterway's naming. Was this unknown hollering woman often heard calling her numerous children in for supper near the creek bed, or was there a more sinister cause for the woman's shrill cries at hand? Were her loud shouts greeted with the laughter of her family eager to sit down to dinner, or was this her last call for help before she encountered her demise? With little written evidence to prove the exact reason for this creek's name, historians have had to rely on folklore passed down through the years.

The oldest and most widely shared description for its naming is a tale told to children in Mexico and the southern United States describing the frightening La Llorona. This loosely translates to "the weeping woman." La Llorona comes from the Spanish verb *llorar*, which means to weep, and the suffix *ona* means great or large and indicates the word is feminine. La Llorona can be translated into "she who weeps copiously," which is precisely what this sad spirit does. Several maps that date from the 1830s give the name Arroyo de la Llorona to this creek now known as Woman Hollering Creek, which gives some credibility to the weeping woman story origin. According to folklore, this gloomy account describes a once young, beautiful and extremely poor woman who was seduced by a wealthy, handsome but married man. Sadly, after being convinced that this man was deeply in love with her and would soon leave his wife, the young woman became pregnant. Shortly after giving birth to their child, she discovered that this deceitful man wanted nothing more to do with her or the newborn. Distraught, confused and in a bizarre attempt to win back the man's heart, she headed down to the creek and drowned the child. The woman, realizing her horrific act of cruelty was a hideous mistake, was grief-stricken, screaming in anguish. She then drowned herself. The tale goes that after her death, the gates of heaven would not allow her to enter without the soul of her child. Her spirit is doomed to haunt the location of this terrible drowning while wailing in misery and searching for her lost child.

Some of the old-timers state that this story was made up by their ancestors merely to get their children home before dark. One must only assume that back then, using tales of haunting ghosts to keep the youngsters in check seemed more humane than a switch at the hands of an angry parent. Supposedly, putting the fear of a female spirit seeking the soul of a child in the minds of youngsters would pretty much guarantee parents that their kids would get home before dark and stay away from the water's edge. It must have worked, because oddly enough, the story of La Llorona and her desire to correct her mistake is one of the most popular and longest-running tales in the Seguin area and even spans into South America and Mexico.

Although there has been an abundant source of individuals who have attempted to accurately reveal the true reason for this creek's gloomy name, no written accounts have been uncovered so far to provide a sound conclusion. Yet ask any true local what they believe is the reason for the strange naming, and they will openly give you what they know to be the truth. These residents will gladly share the trusted tales passed down to them for generations by their ancestors without blinking an eye. Each native approached will eagerly offer up the story told to them by their distant ancestors as though it was simply a part of their family's history. This rare tale has been told so often by their kinfolk that it becomes just a minor fragment of a family's past. One would think that over the many years that have passed, these locals would have grown numb to the brutality of this tale. The reason for their continued sharing of this tale is hard to believe. As unbelievable as it may sound, this illustrious woman is not well known due to the severity of her death. It is her hollering—which continues to this day, although she has long since passed—that makes her so famous. What is even more chilling is that the majority of these locals all offer up the same ending to their story, with the words, "Go stand near the creek at the wee hours of the morning and hear her sad cries, then decide whether you believe or not after that."

Needless to say, this woman's loud yelling was not a joyful calling for her children, after all. In fact, those screams were an excruciating cry for help caused by a horrific episode. This horrendous version of the legend begins in the mid-1800s with an unidentified pioneer woman traveling with a group of settlers who had temporarily made camp by the creek. She made a devastating decision that would change her life forever. Without considering the immense danger of raiding Indians, she decided to go to the small creek alone to either fetch fresh water or to wash her clothes. No sooner than she had arrived at the creek, a large group of Indians, possibly Comanches, quickly surrounded her. One of the Indian braves snatched her up and placed her on his horse. They swiftly began to ride away with this terrified woman as her intense cries for help could be heard by the entire settlement. Her husband and the other men knew this was a kidnapping, and without hesitation, they frantically gave chase to the Indians and the captured woman. Although they desperately tried to reach her, they were greatly outnumbered and knew it was impossible to save her. Knowing that if they rode too far away from the settlement, the other women could be injured as well, they made the painful decision to abandon the rescue. Although the other men begged her husband to return to the settlement with the group, he refused and continued on his doomed path with little hope. They watched him as he disappeared over the horizon and was no longer visible. The men returned to the camp, grieving with the disappointing news of their unsuccessful rescue. All of the settlers crowded together around the campfire with tears in their eyes. Along with their grief and fear for their own lives, they also had to painfully endure the horrific cries for help from the kidnapped woman, who was being brutally tortured. Her screams could be heard for hours, and it was a sound the settlers would never forget. The woman's husband was never seen again, and everyone assumed he, too, met his fate at the hands of the murdering Indians, although his body was never found.

It is said that the woman's cries are an enduring reminder of how difficult it was in the untamed West. On certain early summer mornings, her horrific screams can still be heard on occasion. The shadowy figure of a tall cowboy walking along the banks can also be seen from time to time. Is this her husband, still searching for his bride in hopes of rescuing her? The ghostly white figure of a woman reaching outward as if pointing at something or someone has also been seen in the evenings. Is this the young mother searching for her child she wishes she had not injured? No one will ever truly know the truth behind the naming of Woman Hollering Creek. It is quite possible that both of these tales are correct, for each is easily conceivable. Since these versions have been passed on for generations, there must be some truth to them in some small way. In any case, the accounts of these ghostly figures seem to be appearing more and more often. Many believe it is due to the technical paranormal research devices that are leading the way to more visual and audio confirmation. It may be possible that these devices are making it easier for the spirits to communicate, or maybe they are just finally ready to tell their story.

No one may ever really know the exact truth about the naming of this creek. Nevertheless, be careful while strolling along the banks of the Woman Hollering Creek alone. You just might stumble on some eerie sounds and ghostly sights that could make any grown person go running through the night, crying like a baby.

Chapter 6

THE SEGUIN–GUADALUPE COUNTY HERITAGE MUSEUM

THE POST-SLAVERY POTTERS

The co-founder of the Ripcrew team Wiley Uzzell stated, "No sooner than we walked into the large bottom-floor portion of the building, everyone's K2 meters lit up and the hairs raised up on all our arms. We knew we were in for a wild ride when this happens." This is exactly how the evening began when initiating the first paranormal investigation at the Seguin–Guadalupe County Heritage Museum, located at 114 North River Street in downtown Seguin. The supernatural energy of this building was exhilarating, and the team was anxious to take on this investigation with intense examination. Not one person who entered that building doubted that it was occupied by something paranormal. The team members didn't question whether the building was haunted; that had already been answered just by walking in. Their task at hand for the evening was now to determine who or what was causing the haunting.

This two-story structure with a balcony is an outstanding red brick building constructed in 1898 by Henry Troell, a German immigrant who had moved to this area prior to 1860. It had Victorian-era pressed tin ceilings, pine floors and even original Seguin bricks on the walls. The second floor served as Seguin's Kempen-Stein Opera House for several years, while the bottom floor served as a series of small businesses in the beginning. It housed a haberdashery, a furniture store and a clerical business. It is mostly known for being the Red and White Grocery and the popular S&H Green Stamps Store. When the last store closed, it became Strom's Black Belt Academy and many other different businesses until 1992. This is when the Baenziger family decided to donate the building to a private association if it would transform the structure into a public museum.

In April 1998, the Heritage Museum had its official opening, showing cultural attractions and receiving visitors from all around the United States. This building has a charming historical background but certainly not the type that would generate the forceful paranormal activity that was being registered by the paranormal team. With no recorded deaths, any violent events or even hefty remodeling currently in progress, there was no reason for this type of intense activity. Then someone made the comment that maybe it wasn't one particular spirit lingering within but rather the museum's rotating examples of the area's immigrant and ethnic heritages were causing the activity. It was as though a light bulb went off in everyone's heads. From that point on, everyone focused on the artifacts.

As the team members went from display case to display case, they noticed a certain pattern being formed. All activity was coming from the case housing the Wilson Pottery. The closer and more focused they led their research in that direction, the stronger the evidence developed that this was the source of the energy. The team decided to step outside and discuss the history of this pottery collection with the museum's staff members on hand. They went to great length to correctly explain the incredible history of this stoneware

Before becoming the Seguin-Guadalupe Heritage Museum, the building once housed the Red and White Grocery. *Copyright by the Leon Studio Collection of the Heritage Museum.*

It was also once enjoyed by locals as the S&H Greens Stamps Catalogue store before becoming the Seguin-Guadalupe Heritage Museum. *Copyright by the Leon Studio Collection of the Heritage Museum.*

to allow the team to better understand. It seems this isn't just any normal everyday pottery. It had a fascinating history of a tale from rags to riches–type success.

This amazing account began in 1857, when John McKamey Wilson, a Presbyterian minister, educator and slave owner, established the first Wilson Pottery. His business produced utilitarian alkaline-glazed and salt-glazed stoneware all through the Civil War years. Reverend Wilson was not a potter himself; instead, he hired professional potters to teach his slaves the pottery craft. The actual initial pottery operations were conducted by his slave potters, Hiram, James, George and Andrew Wilson. While the slave Wilsons where still in bondage, they learned the craft and became quite skilled at it. The business flourished and prospered, making a wide variety of vessel forms, such as chamber pots, churns, bowls, pitchers and storage jars to satisfy local needs of that time. When the Civil War finally came along, it severely disrupted the lives of many, including the Wilson slave potters. After the troops went home and the slaves were freed, since the slaves had been so successful while in bondage, it was only logical that they form a similar business now that they were free. This is exactly what they did. The potters at the Wilson Potteries relocated into two separate shops in 1869. One was run by M.J. Durham, John Chandler and Isaac Suttles. The other was run by the former slaves Hiram, James and Andrew Wilson. The latter was renamed Hiram Wilson and Company. It was one of the rare examples of a pottery owned and operated by a freed black man in the nineteenth-century South. Hiram Wilson and Company made only salt-glazed ware and always marked the vessels with the company's name (H. Wilson and Co.), a practice not followed by most contemporaries.

Hiram Wilson assumed a role in Capote, Texas, similar to that of his former master in Seguin. He started a church and a school, as well as the outstanding pottery. The separation of the black Wilsons into a freedman's community may have been a response to postwar violence and general hard feelings by the previous slave owners evident in reports of Freedman's Bureau officers in Seguin. Two instances of violence against the Wilsons were reported in 1867. Hiram Wilson and Company went out of business about the time of Hiram's death in 1884. Some of the men, including James Wilson, then went to work with Durham and Chandler at their pottery, which continued operation until about 1903.

Now knowing the detailed history of this display of pottery, the paranormal team members went back into the building. As they focused their investigation and EVP sessions on the pottery, remarkable effects started to unfold. With each question, there was a reaction in some form. There was banging on the walls and tapping on the counters, and a book was even thrown to the floor. As a group of investigators headed upstairs, the completely unlit building was swiftly brightened by all of the lights being turned on in one instant. Glass shelves from the display cases around the Wilson Pottery exhibit were knocked down to the ground. Disembodied male voices could be heard by the human ear, not needing a digital recorder to distinguish them. The strongest evidence was the K2 meters held by numerous researchers. These meters would reach top-level settings when approaching the pottery.

Once the investigation was over, the team unanimously agreed that the Wilson Pottery was definitely the source of the paranormal activity. The reason for it, though, was not unanimously agreed on. Some felt the pottery was merely sending out strong residual activity that remained behind from the makers' energy put into it. Knowing this pottery was their only source for financial survival, one can only imagine how important this craft was to them. The motivation to succeed had to have been powerful. This is why a few felt it was solely the enduring energy remaining from the pottery, while others felt that the spirits of these talented, durable survivors known as the

Wilson craftsmen were trying to express their presence. They wanted the public to be made aware that they were still as resilient as their long-lasting pottery, even after death. Whatever the case may be, there is no question the Seguin–Guadalupe County Heritage Museum is haunted. Whether it is residual or not, the paranormal energy coming from the Wilson Pottery inside the museum is unquestionable. Stand by the display case to see for yourself. While there, be sure to give a nod of respect to the remarkable freed slaves who beat all odds.

Chapter 7

RIVERSIDE CEMETERY'S WHITE OWL

LEGEND OF LA LECHUZA

There is a solemn yet impressive cemetery in Seguin just south on River Street called Riverside Cemetery. It is known for being the burial place of many of Seguin's Confederate heroes and early settlers. The tombstones are stoic and ornate, giving a sense of going back in time. Each one is precisely designed with great care by loved ones hoping to give the deceased one last sign of respect and devotion. As you arrive, the smell of moss and decaying leaves is overwhelming. Alongside well-kept headstones with flowers newly placed by descendants, there are tumbled and broken tombstones with weathered inscriptions. This cemetery is not only the tranquil burial site for many early Texas settlers, but it is also known as the home base for one of Texas's most foreboding and ancient legends.

This extraordinary cemetery originated as the Smith Family Graveyard. It was established by the initial settlers to this area. Ezekiel Smith, along with his wife, Susanna, and their four sons, came to Texas from Virginia. In 1837, Ezekiel was given a grant of land located in present-day Guadalupe County. One of their sons, French Smith, then deeded the family's cemetery to the City of Seguin. A public cemetery located just north of the Smith Family Graveyard was then founded and later named the Riverside Cemetery. George B. Hollamon deeded an additional piece of land to the city for the cemetery in 1888, and then in 1896, a third tract of land was deeded by W.E. Goodrich. All of these donated cemeteries were eventually combined for a total of fifteen acres. The south side of the cemetery, which faces the Guadalupe River, is forever landmarked by the famous limecrete stone wall, which was built in the late 1800s as one of the small town's defenses. There are nearly two thousand burial sites, including some of the original town settlers, military veterans, noticeable politicians, prominent business leaders, clergymen and even former slaves. Although the city maintained the cemetery at times, over the years, it has fallen into poor condition. In 1994, Friends of Riverside Cemetery took on the task of a complete restoration of the site with the help of volunteer efforts of many concerned citizens and the descendants of those buried in the cemetery. The Riverside Cemetery still continues to serve the community—and one extremely ominous creature.

This esteemed cemetery is a popular stopping point for descendants of the deceased, photographers and historians. Once a year or so, the community holds a living history with costumed actors playing the part and telling the personal stories of those buried here. This graveyard is not only known for its magnificent appearance and history, but it is also a place where some strange sightings have occurred in the midst of silence. It seems that on certain bright full-moon evenings at the Guadalupe River's bottom, there have been some eyewitness accounts of a nearly human-sized white owl. Although oversized owls are not unheard of, what is strange is that this large winged bird appears to have a face resembling a beautiful woman. This unusually enormous feathered female is actually well known in Texas and Mexico, especially to the old-timers. She is called La Lechuza. The Spanish word *lechuza* means an ordinary barn owl, but in this case, she is anything but common.

La Lechuza is essentially a witch who practices black magic. She can turn into an owl and occasionally even additional animal-like forms at night. This enigma has been considered to be a shape shifter, though not evil, but seeing one can be very disturbing, causing one fear. She makes a dreadful, high-pitched screech, sometimes accompanied by a popping and clicking noise. In most accounts of the encounters with this immense feathered witch, she is not so much dangerous as she is frightening, although at times, she does give the impression of having vengeance on her mind and deep hostile business planned. According to the Mexican culture, if you do see La Lechuza, the best way to fend her off is to throw big rocks at her as hard as you can. This will confuse this nuisance's flight or at least drive her from you. You want to keep her as distracted as possible, for it is known that if La Lechuza does not make it back to her place of hiding before morning, she will be stuck in her bird-like appearance for the remainder of the day. This is an event she tries to avoid at all costs. Be warned, though: if you happen to be strolling along during the night and hear the sounds of whistling resembling La Lechuza, it is best that you do not ever whistle back. This mistake could cause you to attract La Lechuza, who will begin her descent toward you and swoop you up. If you have good cause to fear La Lechuza, such as knowingly having upset one, to keep her away from you or your loved ones, lay blessed salt that does not have iodine (known for its purity) around your house as a means of preventing her from entering or attacking you inside.

Legends state that witches are known for practicing both ancient medicine and black magic. They always conduct their business at night, which is why that is when they are most commonly seen. They then bury their incantations in secret hiding places and use their owl-shaped form to make certain these spells remain undisturbed. Legends claims that when La Lechuza locates her victim, she will then perch herself in a remote, tucked-away area near the Guadalupe River and will make her peculiar whistling noises or an uncanny sound similar to the crying of a newborn baby. Her supernatural powers and strength can whisk you away if you have done her wrong. It is even said that two or more Lechuzas will often combine their efforts to work together for either the purpose of good or to prey on those who have done them or someone they know wrong.

The witch-owl's most distinguishing powers are her ability to summons storms, allowing her to direct and control them. It seems that when there is a sighting of this strange fowl, it also coincides with the appearance of tumultuous thunderstorms.

So who could be this extraordinary inhabitant of the Guadalupe River? It is the opinion of many that La Lechuza originates with two well-known factual characters from the book *True Women* by Janice Woods Windle. Once again, it is believed that the famous fortuneteller Idella from the Magnolia Hotel is working her powerful magic. Being such an incredible mystic who could speak to the dead and had an amazing gift for locating things that were considered lost forever, she has been described in Windle's book as "having a soul that floats free in time." Her dearest and closest friend was the man known as Peachtree. He was described as "the raggedy old man who lived in the river bottoms not far from Idella's house." His shack was just a hop, skip and a jump away from the Riverside Cemetery. Peachtree was "a hermit with long, unkempt hair and terrible secrets." He once owned a large white owl, which he kept close at hand with a leather leash attached to its legs. Some say that through the planning of these two mystical people, the white owl was given their supernatural powers when they both passed away. Now the giant snowy-looking bird continues to watch over the area they once called home, monitoring the doings of bad and good that go on along the river. The bird known as Seguin's La Lechuza now resides in the cemetery, guarding over the deceased who once lived and helped build this city.

So beware, as you roam through the majestic Riverside Cemetery, admiring the incredible tombstones and searching for the remnants of the old limecrete wall. Keep a watchful eye around the overgrown trees. If you begin to experience a menacing, closed-in and oppressive feeling, keep in mind that it may not be the spirits of those who once lived. Look to the sky and listen, for it just might be Peachtree's lonely feathered companion keeping a watchful eye on you.

Chapter 8

DEATH OF AN INSPECTOR

MANHUNT TO THE RED RIVER

If you have ever heard of Texas, then you must know of the brave men called the Texas Rangers who protected the range. It seems everyone knows the famous rough-riding lawmen of Texas who were the first team of law enforcement in America. These extraordinarily courageous groups of defenders were actually initiated in 1823, when Stephen F. Austin employed just ten men to take action as the protectors for the newly settled families who arrived in Texas. They were formally organized in 1835, and in close to three years, the Rangers included over three hundred brave men. They were described by Governor Ireland as "a species of moral discipline which developed moral courage. They did right because it was right." From acting as guides and fighting in Indian skirmishes to defending the Alamo, these were the bravest of the brave who watched over the settlers.

Many are unaware, however, that there was another daring and heroic group of lawmen who are rarely mentioned around a story-telling campfire circle or even in Texas history books. These gallant men were known as the Texas brand inspectors. They lived in constant fear of retaliation for simply doing their job of monitoring the cattle and maintaining a level of order in a lawless community, and yet most have been forgotten—that is, except for one inspector who refuses to remain silent, even after his death. This devoted cattle lawman, whose life was cut to short, has still been seen keenly watching over the long-departed ranchers' herds and endlessly observing the distant skyline for rowdy rustlers.

Texas brand inspectors, first called range detectives, are the unsung heroes of the West who quietly kept an eye on an important commodity necessary for the settlers to survive. Without the support of these great men, settlers would have struggled even more than they already did. These vigilante lawmen tirelessly strove to rid the southwestern cattle industry of cattle thievery from 1823 to 1883. They placed their lives in danger on countless occasions to capture rustlers and recover stolen livestock for cattle-raising members. Investigating thefts of cattle, horses and saddles and poaching was a common occurrence. The Texas brand inspectors even carefully inspected livestock to regulate ownership and avoid theft after a natural tragedy such as flood, hurricane or wildfire. Inspectors were ultimately positioned alongside important points of travel, such as cattle trails, market stations and shipping ports. This strategy led to recovering many cattle that by chance or plan got into herds in which they did not belong. These anonymous heroes would determine the ownership of wandering livestock and helped train property owners on how to prevent livestock robbery and squash any possible plans of cattle thieves. Texas brand inspectors played a big part in keeping the peace without all the glory. Many of the lives of these good men were taken too early at the hands of thieving cowards. Their deaths were rarely publicized and seldom vindicated—except for one Seguin inspector, Henry Holmes Batey. Because of a loyalty between two brothers, Batey's death did not go unjustified.

It seems hardworking Mr. Batey was a Texas brand inspector stationed out of Seguin and working diligently during the year of 1877, which was labeled the "big cattle steal" era. The rule about claiming any unmarked cattle was being greatly taken advantage of by crooked rustlers. Because of this, the livestock holders rallied together and formed an association to guard themselves against being robbed of their cows. Guards were positioned on the most frequently traveled routes and at all of the inspection centers, such as the one in Seguin. One of the duties of the brand inspector was to scrutinize the herds for any stolen livestock. On one particular day, Batey refused to allow a herd to continue on with its journey through the county and across the Guadalupe River unless the trail boss granted an inspection. That was the end of the conversation between Batey and the trail boss, and everyone continued on with their duties. About noon, a few hours after the conversation, Batey decided to take a short snooze under the large oak trees close to the intersection of North King Street and East Weinert Street. He lowered the edge of his big cowboy hat to shade his eyes and quickly fell asleep, but sadly, he would not ever wake up again. A man who was riding a gray horse alone came up to Batey while he was quietly sleeping, pulled out his gun and, without blinking an eye, shot him directly in the head.

The news of this horrific event traveled fast, and the town was up in arms. Batey's brother, William Benjamin "Ladd" Batey, was quickly informed of the killing and was devastated. Fuming over his brother's senseless death, Ladd Batey saddled up his horse and headed out on the path of this gutless murderer. All he knew was that the spineless gunman was riding a gray horse. In each small town he passed through, he inquired about the gunman riding a gray horse. Finally, after reaching the Red River, he locked eyes with the killer trying to head for the Indian Territory.

Ladd Batey soon afterward returned to Seguin without saying a word of the results. True to the code of the cattlemen, all he ever eventually said was that he witnessed the cowardly murderer attempting to cross the Red River. Remaining silent thereafter, Ladd Batey never said if the gunman made it to the other side. All those who know Ladd Batey's strong character could only assume justice had certainly been served.

Little did Henry Batey's assassin know that he had chosen to execute one of Seguin's most upright citizens, who held an incredible bond with his devoted brother. It is certain this killer had no idea his heartless decision would eventually lead to both brothers having the last laugh.

The mental and emotional strength of these brand inspectors is unfathomable. Try to imagine, just for a moment, the massive herds of cattle that once meandered down this country thoroughfare with only a handful of men to monitor them. Allow yourself to experience the strength of the imposing livestock in front of you, knowing you are the only law standing between yourself and a possible gutless rustler. Now it is said that if you listen intently at the corner of North King Street and East Weinert Street under the once lush oaks on a soft evening, you can vaguely hear the elusive echoes of the hammering hoofs of herding cattle, the firing of a gun and the sinister laughter of a murdering coward who thought he had gotten away with the perfect crime.

Following the changeover from what was known as the open range to barbed-wire, fenced-in estates, rustling steadily lessened through the great attempts of local area officers, the Texas Rangers and inspectors of cattlemen's associations, who monitored the brands on cattle auctioned off at livestock markets. Though rustling was not completely stamped out, the Texas brand inspectors most assuredly reduced the occurrence. Next time you are in the Seguin area, head over to the Batey's Oaks Historical Marker, where the actual murder was committed. Take off your hat, and offer up a sign of approval to both Henry Holmes Batey and William Benjamin "Ladd" Batey, two brothers fighting for the same cause of pursuing justice, although only one actually carried a badge.

Chapter 9

THE LAW OF THE WHIPPING OAK

SEGUIN'S GROANING TREE

The shackled accused was stripped of his clothing in front of all those who wished to witness the prisoner receive his licks. As his bound arms were raised the sheriff fastened his wrists to the large iron ring implanted in the tree roughly five feet above the ground. The murmuring of the crowd was suddenly silenced as the Sheriff began to raise his four-foot rawhide whip to proceed with the punishment. The lashing of the whip could be heard hitting the bare body of the convicted wife-beater from blocks away. With every whack, whack, whack a painful moan was heard by the accused as he cringed in agony. The crowd which had grown in large numbers flinched with every blow and a slight gasp would follow. The ten strokes were delivered so slowly it took ten minutes to complete. Though no skin was broken, large raised markings were visible.

These are the gloomy words from the *Texas Mercury* newspaper describing what it was like to witness the punishment for crimes in Seguin. Known to the citizens of Seguin as the Law of the Whipping Post, this sentence was feared more than any time in jail or fines assessed. It is an excruciating narrative to hear but a factual account of early Texas pioneer laws. This primitive method of upholding law and order was used on runaway slaves, thieves and wife-beaters. This barbaric form of justice was far more common than one would wish to believe. The consequences of a whipping post were deemed by judges to be far more effective than just sitting in a jail for a few days. For wife-beaters, lawmen agreed that a jail sentence would only cause further hardship to the offender's family. Whipping also seemed to produce better results in lessening future cases.

Very few towns were immune to this brutal method for keeping law breakers in check. Even the pleasant city of Seguin was known to participate in this medieval method of punishment, just inches away from the city's present picturesque gazebo. For those who believe in spirits or have actually seen them, this cruel method of inflicting pain is the reason for the constant ghostly apparitions that often appear in these scenic parts. This area is well known by veteran paranormal researchers for its eerie shadow figures observed as soon as the sun sets.

The sounds of leather used in beatings, painful moans, soft whimpering and even loud wailing have been heard directly across from the south entrance to the Guadalupe County Courthouse in the stillness of a late night. On the north edge of Seguin's Central Park, a collection of gorgeous oak trees stand regal and sound. One of these oaks, in particular, unwittingly stands out among the others, revealing the silent evidence of Seguin's Whipping Oak. Whether all of the trees were once used for punishment by the lash is unclear. Yet at least one has retained proof it was selected by the early court system

The old Seguin Jailhouse. *Copyright by the Leon Studio Collection of the Heritage Museum.*

for the administration of the painful sentencing. Although it remains mute to its past, this grand oak is unknowingly generating paranormal energy from distant times. This unsuspecting voiceless historical object is believed to be where the agonizing audio evidence can be captured. One does not have to be lurking in the dark of the night in Central Park to capture audio evidence. Take any quiet afternoon with a handheld digital recorder and place it near the tree. Countless believers have taken pictures of the iron hook still lodged in the tree with excellent results of a bluish hue surrounding it.

Since 1845, this majestic oak tree has had an iron hook in its trunk, which prisoners were tied to in preparation for their penalty. The exact style in which they were fastened to the tree is not actually known, but the number of lashes was prescribed by the court. On one occasion in 1846, a penalty was assessed by the following sentence: "The guilty shall receive as many licks as given his wife." Occasionally, the sheriff brandished the lash, and at times the court would employ someone else to do the task. These types of public events would always draw large crowds. It would seem the local lawmen actually encouraged a good turnout in hopes of putting the fear of

Front: "Fountain in City Park, Seguin, Texas. 2a1318-N." *Back:* "Seguin was founded in 1838, and was named in honor Col. Juan N. Seguin, a patriot of the battle of San Jacinto. Its principal industries are pecans, cotton, oil, flour, dairy productions, and hydro-electric power generation. It is noted for its parks and municipally owned utilities. Genuine Curteich-Chicago C.T. American Art: Postcard (Reg. U.S. Pat. Off.)" *Author's private postcard collections.*

the whip in people's minds. The courts would even schedule the lashing at lunchtime, allowing spectators to enjoy a picnic during the beating. One can only imagine the oddness of this scene, especially since today it is consider highly abusive to even slightly spank a disobedient child. A reporter for the *Texas Mercury* newspaper overheard an observer state, "The Sheriff did a very nice job though I wish the judge had seen it. Although in my opinion, the Sheriff did not hit him as hard as my own Paw use to hit me!"

Not all settlers regarded the lashing as a fitting punishment for particular crimes, as is evident in an account of one of Seguin's finest, French Smith, who walked by a man bound to the whipping oak. Smith asked what was going on and learned that the man was to be punished for beating his wife. Smith became irate and demanded the man's immediate release, shouting, "That there ain't no fitten crime to be punished for!" I wonder how well that would go over nowadays. So while enjoying a beautiful afternoon in Seguin's Central Park, stroll over to the old Whipping Oak. Place your ear to the bark and allow yourself to imagine how incredibly primitive things were back then. If anything, it will make you grateful for being alive during a more civilized time. Plus, you just might hear the subtle cries of a thoughtless abusive husband vowing to never strike his innocent wife ever again.

Chapter 10

THE HANGING OF HAPPY JACK

THE TOY-MAKING SLAVE

His last words before committing his heinous crime were: "Nicey, you have been telling master a parcel of lies, and damn you, I intend to kill you." To the horror of his master and fellow slaves, he then picked up the nearest axe and hacked his wife to death. What made the scene even more horrendous was that his young wife was eight months pregnant. These horrifying words were taken from the actual district court criminal case files dated November 8, 1860, describing one of Seguin's most brutal and highly confusing murders. The extremely shocking part of this story is that the slave, Jack, who committed this monstrous act was said to have been a religious man who was popular with children, making toys for them in exchange for food. What could cause such a gentle soul to react in such a violent manner? Had he been severely tortured behind closed doors, causing him to finally snap, or had this man been hiding a secret, more sinister side to his personality that was finally exposed? Although his attorney, John Ireland, tried to persuade the courts to appeal their decision, allowing him time to uncover the truth, it would not be permitted. Before the mystery could be solved, Jack's fate was met at the hands of a temporary gallows built on the banks of the Guadalupe River. His death may have silenced the facts as we know them, but it is said that Jack's spirit still yearns to convey his side of the story.

This may come as a surprise, but slavery was actually regulated by a system of laws dating back to the first slave code in 1824. These laws prohibited certain actions that could undermine slavery as an institution, yet they were rarely enforced. In fact, by 1856, the District Court had heard only seven cases against citizens refusing to abide by the laws. Even then, all but one of the indictments was dismissed in the end. Somehow, this doesn't seem like much of a surprise. History has made us painfully aware that much of the punishment for slave offenses was handed out by their masters and certainly not by the courts. Even highly respected citizens such as Green DeWitt, empresario and founder of the famous DeWitt's Colony, had a son, Clinton DeWitt, who was well known for beating and whipping his own wife and abusing his slaves as well. Although he was indicted for the severe abuse in 1847, his case was eventually dismissed. He was ultimately shot and killed by his brother-in-law, Tom Frazier, who had seen his sister suffer for too long. Frazier was then acquitted after being defended by slaves who applauded his actions. One is left wondering if this type of slave owner's lawlessness could be the cause for this once gentle slave known as Jack the Toy Maker to become enraged like a cornered animal.

According to the District Court minutes, slave owner D.A. Word stated, "On the morning of the second day of January, 1860, I took my negro whip and a rope which I used for the purpose of tying negroes to correct them." Word then sent a young slave named Joe to bring Jack in from the fields to his shop. When Jack returned, he saw Word and his wife, Nicey, in the shop and perhaps also saw the whip and the rope. It was then that the toy-making slave Jack went berserk and then murdered his wife and unborn child. The court described his actions as "not having the fear of God before his eyes but being moved and seduced by the instigations of the Devil." Without a doubt, Jack's ghastly deed of murdering his pregnant wife is not in question here, mainly because there were numerous witnesses. This grim act is in no way to ever be excused. The mystery at hand here is what could possibly cause a once gentle person to transform into a monster. In the opinion of many locals and even the paranormal research teams, Jack is still trying to be heard despite the fact that he is no longer living.

This unusual story didn't end when Jack was hanged on December 13, 1861; it actually continues to this day. When Sheriff James McClaugherty stated, "The jail of Guadalupe County not being so constructed that a gallows could be erected within the walls—do hereby convey that a temporary gallows be prepared near the Guadalupe River within the limits of Seguin where at the hour of two o'clock p.m., slave Jack is to be hung until dead, dead, dead," he also generated a tale that would live on for generations. Now it is said that if one heads to the highest point along the riverbank, just a short distance from the old county jail on East Donegan Street, one can still hear the swinging of

Front: "Court house Seguin, Tex. [handwritten] Can't guess where I am? I came home for the carnival am going 'right' balck! I came thankfully Thursday eve. Sorry I didn't get to see you. I'm awfully "blue" so "lonesome." But must hush you might "suspect" something and I wouldn't have you do that for words. Jaime. Monday Oct. 15 '06. Tell Dora Alice she owes me a letter." *Back*: address: Mr. Maurice Dowell. Luling, Texas. Stamp: Seguin Texas Oct. 15, 1906. *Author's private postcard collections.*

the gallows precisely at the hour of two o'clock. Jack has been seen walking along the banks of the Guadalupe River, where a crowd of over 1,500 people came from all around to witness this gentle giant be hanged. The words "he made me" and "listen" have often been heard by the human ear. The most profound sound is the soft male sobbing coming from the trees as if someone were grieving. Often, a tall shadow figure has been often seen searching for something along the river and then quickly disappears.

Is Jack trying to explain his reasons for this terrible act, or was there more to it than what was revealed? Evidently, the esteemed attorney and governor John Ireland felt there was more, for he actually appealed the decision to hang Jack all the way to the Texas Supreme Court but was denied. Afterward, a statement from the court read: "And the jury having ascertained the value of said slave Jack to be twelve hundred dollars, it is ordered that the Clerk prepare the proper documents to enable Mrs. Mary E. Word [who was the actual owner of Jack] to receive from the treasury of the state such part of said value as the law allows her to receive." It is certainly possible that the truth may never be revealed in our lifetime. Yet there is hope for those who continue to believe that answers may still come from beyond the grave through researching and investigating with an open mind. With these types of bold, strong-willed people willing to listen, maybe someday Jack's real story will finally be revealed.

Chapter 11

SEGUIN TRAIN DEPOT

THE LIGHT-WAVING RAILROAD MAN

Most of us know that "a hidden treasure" is a commonly used phrase meaning something beautiful is just a tad out of sight or slightly concealed. This is exactly what awaits you at the corner of North Austin Street and Braden Street, where there is a minor hill alongside the railroad tracks. If you wish to see this incredible secret, pull up along the old crumbling brick curb and park your car. Now walk a short distant up the small mound, staying away from the railroad tracks. Look down and prepare to be astonished. You will be surprised at what you will discover, and thoughts of what it must have been like during its prime will enter your mind. What is this so-called buried gem, you ask? Here is a small hint: the location is precisely one mile from the courthouse, thanks to the strong lobbying by Governor John Ireland. If that doesn't help, then here's another: it brought an end to the stagecoach line. That's right. It is the gorgeous mosaic floor of the original 1910 Seguin Train Depot. Sadly, this is all that is left of this ornate building that was scrapped because of its poor conditions. One can just imagine, though, how exciting this depot area was at one time. With so many people coming and going, it must have been an extremely lively place. But before you head out to stand in the center of this former energetic building and reminisce about days gone by, a fair warning is essential. If visiting after sunset, the sight of lavish decorative flooring and the possibility of a noisy train passing may not be the only surprise you encounter. Some unusual unexplainable activity has been occurring at this location as of late. This leads one to wonder whether the tiled flooring isn't the only thing left behind by the demolition crew.

From train whistles when none are near to shadow figures of past employees, something is definitely being stirred up at this exact spot. Some assume these strange incidents are due to recent talks of rebuilding a replica of the old depot to resemble its once glorious appearance on precisely the same spot. Hope of renovation and reconstruction is a huge trigger for spirits who still linger. Could these odd happenings be ghostly signs of excitement and anticipation of those who once traveled from or worked at the depot? Those who have long since passed must surely recall the exhilaration felt when the railroad finally rolled into Seguin.

It was a long, hard struggle to bring the train to Guadalupe County, and it was greatly needed. Had it not been for one of Seguin's most famous inhabitants, John Ireland, the railroad would never have landed where it is. While Ireland was a member of the Texas legislature, he successfully lobbied for the passing of a law that controlled the laying down of any railroad tracks. The railroad stations could not be more or less than one mile from the town's county courthouses in all counties. If stations didn't comply, there would be consequences. Needless to say, Seguin's first depot, which was just a wooden building then, was exactly one mile from the courthouse.

One mile may not sound very far, but in fact, getting to and from the depot to the inner city was rather rough at times. The path was unimproved, and

Front: "Guadalupe County Court House, Seguin, Texas—4." *Back*: "Made in U.S.A. by C. Kropp Co., Milwaukee, Wis. Photo by Weiss Studio." *Author's private postcard collections.*

Very rare photo of the Seguin Train Depot, which is now long gone. *Copyright by the Leon Studio Collection of the Heritage Museum.*

when it rained, it was a topsy-turvy, muddy challenge. Many of the weary travelers were forced to tread through pastures behind the buildings to get to the town. To make the trip easier, a group of light rails were fitted, and a streetcar service pulled by a mule was put in place in 1886. It ran down the area that is now Austin Street and encircled the city square before heading back to the depot. It made its way down this track in the earlier days before cars were invented, when it was the only commercial transportation in Seguin. The mule-drawn streetcar distributed all the postal service, cargo and travelers entering and leaving town. The entire company was made up of ten mules, a summertime open coach and a wintertime closed coach and four flatcars for carrying freight. Only one single mule was used at a time to pull the car. This quaint form of passage lasted all the way until 1915, when the roads were finally paved. Much of the streetcar tracks can still be seen since the tracks were never actually removed, just paved over. On quiet early Sunday mornings when there is no city traffic, youngsters have said you can still feel the rumble of the rails when touching them, as if they are still in use.

Seguin experienced a deeply needed financial improvement in the mid-1870s, when the assembly of the Galveston, Harrisburg and San Antonio

Photo of Seguin Street Railway, used to provide transportation from the train depot around town. *Copyright by the Leon Studio Collection of the Heritage Museum.*

Front: "Seguin Street Railroad, Seguin, Texas." *Back*: "San Antonio, 4/12/12. The reverse is the sole rolling stock of the Seguin Railway Co. Leaving Street. Here at 4:45 for Comfort. Alfred." Address: Mrs. M. Wacker Barlett Tecas" 8011—P.E. Serger, Publisher, Seguin, Texas. Stamp: Houston San Anton R.P.O. Apr 12 1912. *Author's private postcard collections.*

Railway began. The railroad made its way to Seguin in 1876 en route to San Antonio. This gave Guadalupe County residents easier access to markets. Area farmers were able to sell livestock for top dollar and eliminated the danger involving extensive cattle drives. Cotton soon became the foremost crop after the county recuperated from the dreadful Civil War and forceful Reconstruction. By 1879, there was an eastbound and a westbound daily train leaving out of Seguin. There was even a telegraph operator. The railroad changed Seguin from just a small stop on a stagecoach route into a bustling city. The first original wooded depot is believed to possibly have burned down, and the more ornate one was then built around 1910. The old freight depot is actually still standing just down the way and is an active feed store.

Of course, over time, the practice of passenger travel changed, and the railroad was replaced with the popular automobiles. Yet there was one last burst of use for the railroad at the start of World War II. Thousands of soldiers and military equipment were transferred by the nation's railroads. Imagine all of the soldiers having to say goodbye to their loved ones at this depot, not knowing if they would return.

After the war, passenger service was canceled, and the depot eventually closed. After many years of the depot remaining empty, the building gradually fell into disrepair. The once vibrant depot became an eyesore, attracting undesirables, and something had to be done. Unfortunately, the structure was a large, complex, masonry building, making it difficult to be moved. Unable to easily relocate it, the city reluctantly allowed the railroad to demolish the depot in the late 1980s. Recently, more and more people have claimed to hear the sounds of a large cast-iron steam whistle, similar to those once on a locomotive. It seems the swinging of a hand lantern can be seen at the crossing, as if warning of an approaching train. The small but plump figure of a man wearing a tall hat and holding what appears to be a pocket watch has been seen several times. Even the modern railroad arms have been seen mysteriously going down to stop traffic when no train is anywhere near. Have these spirits been quietly haunting the sparse remainder of the depot that was demolished many years ago and only now are people speaking of their encounters? Or has the talk of a possible replica of the depot being constructed brought these spirits renewed excitement? If you are brave enough, next time you see an old-timer carrying a pocket watch by the railway, ask him when the next train arrives. Word of caution, though: be wary if he responds with an "all aboard" yell and a ghostly train then appears. It might be best if you decline.

Chapter 12

THE HEADLESS WALKER

DEATH OF A GENERAL

Just about everyone in Seguin has heard the tale of the headless ghost whose nightly walks begin near the Guadalupe River around the River Drive East area and continue through Riverside Cemetery onto South Milam Street, ending on North Milam Street at the railroad. The man, who has remained nameless all these years, is rumored to be an unsuspecting Confederate private who was misfortunate enough to have had his head shot off by a cannonball during some skirmish in the east. This version has been examined often since there is no actual record of such a hideous accident happening to a soldier or even of a battle in that area. Another conflict to the story is that the war was over in 1865, so had the soldier been killed during this war, he would not have even known about the train since it was not built until 1877. Since the headless walker has been seen by many for generations, no one questions the ghost's existence; to locals, he is a genuine resident. The real question here is who is this headless ghost? Although this depiction does make for a ghastly and shocking Halloween-type tale, it is lacking substantial proof. However, there is a strong indication that this poor wandering soul does have a name and a factual story behind him.

It seems the possibility of the headless strolling spirit being a Confederate soldier may be true to some degree, for this ghost was once a general in the Civil War. This gallant man was described as "a brave and true soldier" who had served in Company K of the Eighth Texas Infantry under Lieutenant Colonel John Ireland of Seguin, Texas, for three years and nine months. Even though he had been of high stature in the local social and business world, he suffered a silent pain for years. His quiet agony finally took its toll and caused this once tough soldier to eventually take his own life. Who was this mysterious gallant man now assumed to be the headless walker? It is General William Saffold, considered to be the wealthiest man in 1860, according to the tax rolls in Guadalupe County.

The obituary in the *Seguin Enterprise* of Friday, August 7, 1896, was titled "A Very Sad Ending," and it stated: "General William Saffold, age 68 ends his days of suffering with his own hands. He leaves letters giving cause for the deed. About half past nine o'clock yesterday morning news came to town that General Saffold had committed suicide at his home near the Guadalupe River." The *Enterprise* reporter then set out to obtain the facts of the sad affair and presented the following:

> *The General arose at his usual hour and partook of a hearty breakfast, and had his buggy hitched up as usual, for a ride in the country. About nine o'clock his nephew, Mr. John Dwyer who is here on a visit from Waco went to his room and knocked at the door which was found locked. He was admonished by his uncle from within, not to disturb him, but sent up the colored boy, Perry Mack. When the boy appeared he made known the fact that he had attempted to take his own life, and was then suffering from a wound in his left side inflicted by a long blade knife, and requested the boy to notify his niece, Mrs. Z.T. Beasley, who with her two children [sic]. Miss May was also on visit to him from Waco and to summons [sic] a physician, but to have no fears as everything was all right. The boy departed and before an investigation could be made, the repost of a pistol was heard in his room. The spectacle which met the eye of the persons who entered was his form lying on a carefully prepared pallet on the floor. He had placed the pistol, a .45 caliber, to his right eye and fired. The ball ranged diagonally and came out the left side of the head—tearing away the entire front portion of the scull leaving him nearly headless. Pieces of brain and scull [sic] were splattered on the floors and walls. He expired in a few minutes. General William Saffold's remains are to be by a San Antonio firm and shipped to his old home in Newton, Newton County, Mississippi.*

This account was very painful for the small town of Seguin to hear, for William Saffold had been deeply respected. He had been a major landowner and local merchant and even had a dam built in Seguin. Saffold had built his house in 1865 as soon as he returned from the war; in fact, it still stands to this day. In addition to his service in the war, he was on many committees in town, had his own store on the town square and saved the schools in town from going bankrupt. According to his family, it was said that many famous people stayed with him in his home, though they never mentioned any particular names.

In William Saffold's obituary in the newspaper, he was described as

having accompanied his father Byrd Saffold to Guadalupe County in 1854. The family stood high in social circles in Mississippi and joined the tide of the better classes who came and settled here from the old states about that time. They were possessed of considerable means and were looking for a new country to be paid, this they found in Guadalupe County. At his father [sic] death, Mr. Saffold fell heir to his ample estate. He has managed it with the skill of a Rothchild. He made loads [from] his principal investment, and each year added to his principle [sic]. At his death he was probably the wealthiest man in the county. Honesty and integrity coupled with sound judgment were his chief supports in business affairs. For the

Front: "Power Plant, Dam and Falls on Guadalupe River, Seguin, Texas. 9a69-N." *Back*: "Seguin was founded in 1838, and was named in honor Col. Juan N. Seguin, a patriot of the battle of San Jacinto. Its principal industries are pecans, cotton, oil, flour, dairy productions, and hydro-electric power generation. It is noted for its parks and municipally owned utilities. Genuine Curteich-Chicago C.T. American Art: Postcard (Reg. U.S. Pat. Off.) [Handwritten] Dear Nancy, Here's hoping you've had a pleasant summer and that I'll be seeing you soon. Love, Miss Zinnell." Address: Miss Nancy Calhoun. 207 E. Pepron City. Stamp: San Antonio, Texas 052. Aug. 19 5 PM. *Author's private postcard collections.*

past 25 years he has been suffering from cancer, which terribly mutilated his face and as his note to the Enterprise *explains, caused intense suffering and loss of sight. The news of his death will be received with sorrowful surprise by his large circle of acquaintances and friends, who upon [being] apprised of it will be reminded of the old axiom, that contentment blessed with health is the greatest gain of all.*

Evidently, William Saffold was not alone among his kinfolk in suffering from depression. He came from a long line of deeply disturbed members of his family. It seems two of his cousins on his mother's side, Allen and Drew Cade, took their own lives later in life, and his paternal aunt, Mary Saffold Barnett, was declared legally insane and made a ward of William's father, Bird Saffold. It is also known that there were several other deaths that occurred in the original Saffolds home, though these were rarely spoken of. Is it just a coincidence that the known route of the headless walker happens to begin where William Saffold took his own life and ends at the railroad station where his body was removed to Mississippi? Or is this finally the proof needed to say that William Saffold is indeed the mysterious headless walker? It is the opinion of many that this is the residual energy of a great man who could no longer bear the pain he had to endure every day, yet he hated to leave the city he once loved.

Even in his last words, he declared his love for his friends, reading books and social gatherings. This letter is the actual words written in a clear hand by William Saffold that was delivered to the office of the *Enterprise* newspaper with a request to publish it as an advertisement. It proves that everything about his death was prearranged:

To my friends in Seguin, Texas on Aug. 6, 1896. To be or not to be that is the question; whether 'tis better in the mind, to suffer the slings and arrows of outrageous fortune, Or to take arms against a sea of troubles and by opposing, end them. A word to my friends may not be out of place. With ample fortune and at peace with mankind, I am and have been, for some years, to a considerable extent a hermit, by reason of circumstances beyond my control, depriving me of the sweet converse of my friends and the pleasures of society—this enforced imprisonment has been borne, I trust with stoic fortitude. But now, I am confronted with the loss of sight; which through these long years has been my best and truest friend, enabling me with books, periodicals and correspondence to keep somewhat in touch with the times. Now, ere this us [sic] obscured forever, rendering this beautiful world with its changing lights and shades a dreary waste, I fain would bid it and my friends a long farewell.

Judge Jas. Greenwood shows the high esteem in which General Saffold was held by his old friends who knew him for years by stating to the *Enterprise* newspaper, "I always liked William Saffold. There was a steady firmness, a strict integrity visible in all of his dealings. Then he was courteous and kindly in his manner towards his friends. He had none of the old man's [his father] jolly humor and boyish ways, but his energies and thoughts were all the time on the financial line. He was a true friend; an honest man. Such he showed himself to be in those olden days. And you have known him well since then."

If you see an apparition of a stoic man in his late sixties headed toward the old railroad station from the river, merely tilt your hat in admiration or offer up a slight curtsy, reminding this once honorable man that he is still respected. Though having lived his life as honorably as possible, life just happened to deal him a bad hand, causing him to make a choice he must endure even to this day.

Chapter 13

LAKE MCQUEENEY

THE GUARDIAN OF THE LAKE GHOST

There is a part of Guadalupe County that rarely gets mentioned when discussing paranormal experiences, most likely because it is a place of fun, sun and recreation. However, no matter how pleasurable a place may seem to those who visit, spirits may still linger among us for reasons unknown. This is just the case with Lake McQueeney. Locals, tourists and passersby for years have seen yet seldom speak of the thick white misty figure that appears over the water during the threat of a possible flood. This hazy-looking, snowy-colored spirit has been spotted since the mid-1900s. Locals who have come across the floating silhouette have come to rely on this credible vision as a warning of high water being likely. Though the thought of a ghostly mist appearing ever so often is rather spooky, locals have fondly deemed it a protector. This spirit that simply wishes to warn the people in the area of the potential risk of a flood has been nicknamed the Guardian of the Lake.

How this spirit came about and whom it might be are burning questions; with all the suicides and horrendous flood victims on the lake, no one can actually pin down the name of this caring spirit. So who could this caring messenger be who wishes only to alert the community of imminent danger? The list is somewhat lengthy and intriguing and begins rather far back in time. Some believe the spirit was an unsuspecting member of one of the Indian tribes that often camped along the river who might have fallen victim to the quick rising waters. Although the area tribes, such as the Tonkawas, were well aware of the river's potential for devastating fury at any moment, the Guadalupe River can take even the most experienced by surprise. How frightening it must have been to be so close to a river and not know how to swim. Regrettably, it was all too common for even a strong warrior to be swept away by the strength of the river's raging currents. It is quite possible the spirit may be an Indian warrior wishing to warn his fellow tribe members to be more wary of the river's power.

Others believe it is one of Colonel Joshua Wright Young's numerous slaves buried on the property he once owned. Colonel Young came to the area around 1850 with nearly two dozen slaves. He was the creator of the Seguin Sebastopol and owned several cotton plantations located on both sides of the Guadalupe River. Young's coastal prairie land had a narrow area on his property that crossed the river. That low water crossing known as a ford became a major transit point for generations of pioneers and settlers. Before the Civil War, Colonel Young would bury his slaves who had passed away near the west end of that ford. Unfortunately, after the dam was in place, the river would rise near the burial site, and the water would open the graves. The bones of these forgotten departed would have to be retrieved by local children, no less, and then reinterred. It is a well-recognized paranormal fact that spirits will become restless if not given a proper burial or if their site is disturbed. It would seem that having your bones washed away by the water and then improperly reinterred by kids would definitely qualify as unsettling.

Then there are those who believe it is an officer of the Texas Hydro-Electric Corporation and Guadalupe Water Power Company named Gerald Peck, who was shot to death by a disgruntled farmer. Peck happened to be president of the company at the time and had nothing to do with the dam's design. This displeased farmer was none other than Seguin's Tom Holloman Sr. While Peck was visiting from Chicago for a routine annual directors meeting, Holloman learned he was in town and broke in on the meeting. He demanded compensation for damages caused by a flood at his property, known as Holloman's Bottom. Holloman was convinced that the harm done to his farm by the waters of the lake was the fault of the Power Company and was seeking reimbursement. Senator Wirtz and F.S. Hunt were present at the time and were part of the confrontation. *Time* magazine on March 12, 1934, stated, "Holloman started to leave after a friendly conversation, wheeled, then fired twice." All that was achieved from this shootout was the death of Peck, and then Holloman died before even going to trial. Many believe Holloman went after the wrong person to begin with because Wirtz was eventually driven out of Seguin from his inappropriate business handling. Could the spirit be Gerald Peck continuing his duties as president of the power company and watching over the dam? Maybe the wispy spirit is Tom Holloman Sr. silently remaining to continue pursuing his settlement and maintaining his watch over the farm.

Of course, there is the possibility that the spirit is the one person who had invested the most time, care and money into the area to help it financially prosper. There is a town near the lake that looks pretty much the same as it did in 1900. It is rather small in comparison to most, but it had the possibility of becoming a very productive stopping point for the railway at one time—at least that is what one of Seguin's most productive entrepreneurs, C.F. Blumberg, was hoping for. Blumberg, who was originally part of the Mainzer Adeslverin group of German immigrants whose family settled originally near Schmansville just south of New Braunfels, had great plans and high hopes for the town he named McQueeney.

McQueeney is just a short distance from Lake McQueeney (also called Lake Abbott) and is located on Farm Road 78. This quiet town dates from 1870, when industrious German settlers moved to the area. Around 1876, the Galveston, Harrisburg and San Antonio Railway was built through the area, and the stop was named Hilda. In 1900, ambitious businessman C.F. Blumberg built a small store one mile east of the rail stop, calling the area McQueeney. This was Blumberg's transparent attempt to persuade the railroad to move the original railroad stop from Hilda to his establishment by designating the town's name in honor of the superintendent of the Southern Pacific line, Mr. McQueeney. Although the railroad never did move the stop from Hilda to Blumberg's store site, he continued to forge ahead and opened a post office (which is now Blake's Café), and the name McQueeney was retained. Could the guardian ghost be Blumberg, still seeking the grandeur he so desired for his small town?

Lastly, there is the tiny likelihood the protector of the lake ghost could possibly be the person who struggled the hardest to get the dam built. This person with such enormous vision was Julius M. Abbott, who for years had dreamt of damming the Guadalupe River to generate hydroelectric power. He began his quest in the early 1900s while living in McQueeney. Though Abbott's huge mission would eventually become a reality, sadly he would not live to see it. In 1927, across the Guadalupe River, the Abbott Dam was completed and provided hydroelectric power to the area, just as he had hoped. The reservoir was then completed in 1928, making it Lake McQueeney in a ceremony for which Abbott's two sons were present. It would seem appropriate for a spirit to wish to linger in the one place that meant so much to him. The dam was the brainchild of Julius Abbott, and without his determination, the beautiful Lake McQueeney that so many now enjoy would not exist. It seems only fitting for Abbott to wish to remain near his greatest achievement.

After the reservoir was built, it was first called Lake Abbott, and it is unclear how or when the lake's name was changed to Lake McQueeney. It went on to become a popular area for recreation and for years has been considered the waterski capital of Texas. This enjoyable area has prompted the building of many lakehouses and summer residences around the lake. There is even a prominent upscale development of homes called Treasure Island. Though there have been numerous damaging floods, such as the ones in 1972 and 1998, the residents continue to rebuild. It is that gorgeous, serene lure of Lake McQueeney that keeps bringing them back. No wonder the lake has a spirit that wishes to remain. Even though the identity of Lake McQueeney's spirit is unknown, it is certain his goal is to protect the people in the area. With his accurate sense of impending high water, it is advisable that you heed his warning if you see a white mist beckoning you to take shelter. There is no reason to be frightened of the spirit, for he is there to monitor your safety. The only real thing to worry about is whether you will be capable of reaching higher ground before the flood comes. One thing is certain: if you see this caring spirit, be sure to give him a huge word of thanks, for he just might have saved your life.

Chapter 14
SEBASTOPOL HOUSE HISTORIC SITE

THE WEEPING WOMAN

A s you walk into this unusually shaped building, the first things you will notice are the relics collected within the building of the past residents' humble means. Their simple way of living is reflected by the sturdy yet worn fixtures on exhibit in several rooms. The displays of tattered photos and relics found during Texas Parks and Wildlife Department diggings and renovations in the 1980s provide insight into the families who lived at the Sebastopol for more than a century. Yet without a doubt, it is not the items that are fascinating to the visitors: it is this unique building itself that draws people in. For some, the true historical artifact they hope to encounter is the presence of the weeping ghost that lingers within the grand walls of this building. Though the house now serves as a playground for enjoyable events for young and old, the weeping woman's sounds of sadness can be heard even through the most delightful of times.

This imposing four-thousand-square-foot white dwelling is one of the limecrete structures of the original register of cisterns, fences and buildings existing in 1900, when Seguin was labeled the "Mother of Concrete Cities." Anyone who is paranormal savvy knows that limecrete is a huge conduit for generating and maintaining hauntings within these types of ghost-magnet walls. With Sebastopol being a solid limecrete structure, many paranormal investigators assumed the building would be haunted, and they were right. This was no surprise at all to the curator of the Sebastopol, for whom unfamiliar noises and strange goings-on were a daily happening. Mysteriously, though, the melancholy sounds of the weeping woman began only recently. Who is this gloomy female, and what is she trying to communicate?

This building is not only recognized for its unusual ghostly occupant, but it is also acknowledge for its strange architect. Sebastopol has been recognized by *Ripley's Believe It or Not* as being one of the very first "air-conditioned" homes in Texas. It has an unusual rooftop construction designed to collect water, which resulted in natural evaporative cooling. Interestingly, though, visitors who look at the house from the ground level see what only appears to be a flat-roofed building, but in fact, this is simply an ingenious architectural sleight of hand. The pitched cedar-shake rooftop is concealed behind the tops of the large Greek columns.

Sebastopol's limecrete construction and architecture are not all that make this building well known. Its odd Greek Revival design makes it a shrine to the middle-class way of life in the nineteenth century. Just like many of the remaining historic structures in Seguin, everything used in constructing the building came from within a sixty-mile radius. All the water, wood, lime and gravel came from Seguin and the nearby area. The one item that had to be brought in was the glass needed for the windows.

Sebastopol's name is believed to have come from the Russian naval base during the Crimean War, though this is not certain. It was erected on a hill above Walnut Branch Creek and sits on 2.2 acres of the original 4.0-acre tract. In 1854, Colonel Joshua W. Young Sr. began building the home for his wife, Jane Field Young. Sadly, she passed away before it was completed. Once it was completed in 1856, Young then sold the house to his recently widowed sister, Catherine Young LeGette. This massive white building was designed be the architect Tobias Meininger. The backbreaking job of building it was then accomplished by the numerous slaves owned by Colonel Young. The limecrete construction used was the famous mixture invented by Seguin's Dr. John E. Park. The very wise Colonel Young insisted on the wide shaded porch that wraps around the building, fourteen-foot-high ceilings and one-foot-thick walls to escape Texas's scorching summer heat. These three inventive cooling systems' designs actually made the building somewhat comfortable. Below ground level, there was a very unusual storage room resembling the appearance of a jail. So far no one has been able to discover its purpose. Catherine Legette remained living at the Sebastopol for nearly twenty years with her children, grandchildren and even Young's other sibling. She then sold it to Joseph Zorn Jr. and his young family in 1874.

Zorn was a Civil War veteran and merchant and was extremely active in the community's growth. He was a direct force in the transformation and modernization of Seguin. He first served as the alderman and then postmaster before he was elected mayor in 1890. Zorn served as Seguin's mayor for twenty years. Under his strong leadership, the town secured water, electricity and even telephone services. Zorn's most significant contributions were in the area of schooling. In 1891, he demanded an election to create a managed trustee and a free public school system. Seguin residents then made Zorn the first president of the board of trustees. By the end of his term in 1907, the neighborhood had built five new schools. Zorn and his wife, Nettie, had six children together. Their youngest child, Calvert, continued to live in the Sebastopol until 1952. After Calvert's passing, the home was leased out for a time by a local Seguin family. Around the 1960s, the building was uninhabited, in disrepair and slated for demolition.

Thankfully, the Seguin Conservation Society bought the property and began restoring the façade of the building. It operated it as a museum until 1976. It soon became obvious that the substantial structural repairs needed were way beyond the scope of the Seguin Conservation Society's capabilities. The Texas Parks and Wildlife Department then stepped in to preserve this historic home. Texas Parks and Wildlife purchased Sebastopol for the amount of $750,000 from the Seguin Conservation Society in 1976, and extensive restoration was undertaken. The house was stripped down to its walls and rough framing. The original pine, cypress, box elder, elm, oak and walnut framing was removed, labeled and stored for future replacement. The contractors then stabilized the collapsing limecrete walls using the same original type mixture of sand, gravel, lime and rock excavated from the site. Interior and exterior walls were replastered and completed in historically correct colors and coatings. Sebastopol was again opened to the public in September 1989. The building is restored to its grand 1880s appearance. In 2011, ownership was transferred to the City of Seguin. Exhibits on display describe the original construction, the intense restoration process and the history of the home and its previous residents. Certain Zorn and LeGette family items are exhibited indicating the decor of middle-class families who lived there in the late nineteenth century.

With this building having a rather normal background with residents who seemed to have enjoyed their time there, who could this weeping woman be? Some believe it is Colonel Young's wife, Jane, who passed away before even living in the building her husband was so lovingly having built for her. There is also Catherine Young LeGette, who was widowed at a young age with numerous children. Maybe she wishes she could have shared the Sebastopol with her dearly departed husband. Then there are the painful times of

Reconstruction after the Civil War, when soldiers would commandeer the larger, grander homes for their own use and steal all of the belongings. Though not recorded, this type of personal invasion was more common than we would like to believe. Could this have happened to Catherine's home during that time, leaving her grieving for the loss of her property? Some believe it is the sadness of one of Colonel Young's female slaves because the words "trapped," "owned" and "freedom" have been captured by several paranormal teams' EVP sessions. Did she pass before the Civil War ended and still seeks that personal independence?

This building requires further investigation if a solid answer is truly sought. For now, the weeping woman's sounds are being soothed by the verbal comfort of the visitors who are aware of her. Until the reason for her unhappiness is discovered, maybe next time you visit the museum, you could give her a word of reassurance. Let her know you are aware of her sadness and that if she wishes to share her grief, you are willing to lend her an ear. Give her hope by letting her know there are numerous caring paranormal believers out there who are continuing to uncover how to provide her with peace. Someday this mystery will be solved, her cries will stop and the Sebastopol will again be filled with laughter, as it once was when the Legette children and grandchildren lived there.

Chapter 15

MARY B. ERSKINE SCHOOL

THE DISCIPLINARIAN GHOST

It appears this publication would not be complete unless the ghost of the Mary B. Erskine Elementary School was included. According to numerous local youngsters, this building is considered to be the most recognized haunted building in Seguin. The school's ghost seems to have taken up residence there since the mid-1900s, allowing for this tale to be repeated for several generations. Although the Ripcrew team did not investigate this building, given its vast notoriety in the Seguin paranormal realm, it just would not be appropriate unless the tale of this building's ghost was mentioned.

This spirit has been described as appearing in several forms. One witness stated it appeared as a dark shadow looking back at her in the mirror. Another explained that the spirit was a "shadow-looking white thing" that just stared at her as she combed her hair. Then there are the numerous accounts of an actual apparition resembling a kind but disciplined-looking older woman. There have even been instances where her sudden appearance in the girls' bathroom has left groups of teenaged girls running wildly out the door screaming. Teachers had to come calm down the frightened girls before they could return to class. According to legend, locals feel they know exactly who this hall-monitoring spirit is and openly state it without hesitation. They believe it is the same person for whom the building is named, Mary Browne Erskine. So who exactly is this woman who was greatly honored by having a school named after her and is believed to still be lingering in the halls even after death?

Erskine was fondly recognized by her numerous students as "Miss Mamie." Erskine was born on November 17, 1866, in Belmont, Texas. Her

"High School. Seguin, Texas. Back: C.T. Double tone. AD-12917." *Author's private postcard collections.*

grandfather was none other than Michael Erskine, who once owned the Magnolia Hotel and who bought the José de La Baume Ranch located in the well-known Capotes area. He conducted the initial 1854 cattle drive all the way to California. Mary Erskine's family relocated to Seguin, where she would spend the rest of her life. She attended General Jefferson's Montgomery Institute, an all-girls school, when she was just a young woman. She knew early on that she wanted to become a schoolteacher. At that time, a college education was not required to teach, though Erskine was required to pass a test. Her outstanding personality helped greatly in acquiring the position. All those who knew Erskine respected her principles and values. She was quickly appointed to be the main teacher of the first high school, which opened in 1894. That school was located on the same site as the present Mary B. Erskine Elementary School. At the time, it was called the Seguin High School and housed all grades. The first- through sixth-grade students attended downstairs, with the high school students upstairs. Several years later, Erskine was hired as the principal while still performing her other duties as teacher.

Miss Mamie became an outstanding teacher. Her teaching of phonics and memory work helped her first-grade students excel quickly. Erskine was skilled in keeping her students in line throughout the day. She was a firm disciplinarian and required her students to obey the rules required of them while in school. This would account for the stern-looking ghostly apparition that has been described. By no means was she ever unkind, just extremely direct, orderly and disciplined. It has been said that her favorite phrase was "Just and Right." The children must have appreciated Erskine's upfront attitude and organized way since, in 1922, an issue of the high school's newspaper called *The Cricket Chirps* was devoted completely to her by the students.

Erskine biggest goal was to communicate to the children that it was important to honor not only themselves but also their state and country. She used her own experiences as an example, telling them how when she was a teenager she contributed all of her pennies she had saved to help build the Washington Monument located in Washington, D.C. She was deeply proud of this effort on her part. Erskine encouraged her student to do the same by collecting pennies for them to contribute to Houston, Texas's San Jacinto Monument that was being built. Erskine was extremely active in her church, St. Andrew's Episcopal Church, where she even taught Sunday school.

Though she never married, Erskine was loved by everyone. She lived in her parents' home with her sisters and brothers until her death on June 27, 1926. Seguin demonstrated its devotion and appreciation for this caring teacher the day she passed away. The day of her funeral, all of Seguin's businesses closed, and the town's flags were lowered to half-mast.

After learning of her past and the lengthy time she spent in this building, it is understandable that her name might come up as the possible spirit. It would seem that this charming lady spent a great deal of time in this school that she loved, and she cared deeply for the students. One could understand why she would wish to continue to linger within the walls of a place she sincerely cherished. It is the opinion of most that Miss Mamie Erskine is simply continuing her responsibilities of looking after her students and monitoring the building she deeply treasured. It makes one wonder, though, what the group of girls might have been doing in the school's bathroom that caused Erskine to give them a scare big enough to scoot them out.

AUTHOR'S CONCLUSION

Why do you think ghosts haunt? This has become the most common question asked of me after writing several books on ghosts. In my opinion, there are numerous reasons for this, but the best way I can explain it is that we are all merely spirits enclosed within a physical, flesh-covered body. When we eventually pass, our spirits simply continue on to our next destination. Where that selected destination may be is decided on by our creator and based on how we lived our lives and whether we have any unfinished business left behind. If one has lived a decent, honest life, then it may be possible to request where to spend our eternity, creating one's own view of heaven. Hanging out with my best canine buds Bernie and Saint Francis of Assisi while helping them guard over current earthbound animals in need is my kind of heaven, while others may wish to stay at a place where they had strong emotional ties. They may choose to linger in a small quaint Colorado town surrounded by mountains, sail on the ocean, fish on a Texas pier or remain in a concert hall listening to bands play and inspiring their drummers. This is why I believe we see spirits near beautiful places, not just in creepy-looking buildings. If one has lived a good, moral life, it seems it would be rather generous to be allowed to remain with people or places we loved the most before or even after we have passed. Some spirits may be given an opportunity to complete some unfinished business on earth, such as solving a crime after falling victim to a murder or helping to complete a task they weren't able to finish while still living. I believe it is also possible to stay earthbound to protect a family member in need, which is why some people have guardian angels always by their side. Although everyone has his or her own opinion of life after death, this is mine, and no one will ever really know until our own passing has come.

So what is truly the answer to why ghosts exist? As of right now, there is no substantial proof of *why*—only that they truly do exist. I have felt their presence, heard their voices and sensed their emotions. I have even been guided by a young child to share her final secret. I do not fear death or the presence of spirits. A spirit is merely a soul without a shell wishing to communicate or help in some way. I will always keep an open mind, listen to what they are trying to tell me and continue to help them in any way I can. I hope you do the same. If you are ever confronted by a spirit, please don't run away. Give it a chance to express what it needs of you. Remember, that could be you someday, seeking support from those who still remain living on earth. Happy haunting!

Front: "German Methodist Church, Seguin, Tex. W.C. Kropp, Milwaukee." *Back*: stamp: Seguin Texas Jul 24 4 PM 1907. "July 24, 1907. We are all well yet and hope the same of you all. I went along fishing. From Daniel." address: Mrs. F.J. Hoffmann. R.F.D. #2 Marion Texas. *Author's private postcard collections.*

Old receipt found during restoration at the Magnolia Hotel of the T&E Tractor & Implement Co., 115 South Crocket Street, Seguin, Texas, 1930. *Author's private collection.*

Old receipt. *Author's private collection*

Revised Electric Rates
City of Seguin

Effective With Oct. 1, 1941, Billing

RESIDENTIAL RATE:

FIRST 35 K.W.H. @	7c
NEXT 65 K.W.H. @	3c
BALANCE @	1.5c
MINIMUM BILL	$1.00

COMMERCIAL RATE:

FIRST 35 K.W.H. @	7c
NEXT 165 K.W.H. @	5c
NEXT 400 K.W.H. @	3c
BALANCE @	1.75c
MINIMUM BILL	$1.00

Important:

10% will be added to the bill if not paid by the 10th of the month. All unpaid balances m u s t be paid to avoid payment of the penalty.

Left: Old receipt of the Seguin Electric Rates during 1941. *Author's private collection.*

Right: Weiss Garage receipt from 1958. *Author's private collection.*

Tabulation of GENERAL BIDS FOR SEGUIN ELEMENTARY SCHOOL SEGUIN, TEXAS 4:00, 10 November 1949

Fehr & Granger Architects

BIDDER	BASE BID	WORKING DAYS	Conc.Slab ALT. #1	Joistile ALT. #2	Cement Flr. ALT. #3	Asph.tile ALT. #4	Rubber tile ALT. #5	Alum.sash ALT. #6	12 x 12 acous. ALT. #7	24 x 24 acous. ALT. #8
John Broad	188,723.00		+525.00	1235.00	7200.00	725.00	1375.00	4450.00	1150.00	1675.00
R. B. Butler	115,874.00	160	4320.55	2318.60	6564.55	588.35	1608.00	3585.00	2000.00	2544.25
Leslie Crockett	124,000.00	200	—	+800.00	5500.00	400.00	1400.00	2600.00	1500.00	2100.00
Commercial Con.	164,556.00	185	1015.00	—	4261.00	516.00	1586.00	476.00	1659.00	1967.00
W. R. Davidson	133,700.00	160	1300.00	—	6000.00	400.00	1350.00	6600.00	2100.00	2950.00
Walter Droemer										
Harold Eitze	123,924.00	220	900.00	—	4800.00	500.00	1260.00	2500.00	950.00	1400.00
Archie Fitzgerald										
Rex D. Kitchens										
H. H. Moeller	131,335.00	200	1700.00	100.00	6500.00	350.00	1300.00	6300.00	2000.00	2800.00
Rambo Construction	151,540.00	140	3641.00	550.00	4660.00	470.00	1404.00	3501.00	1415.00	1890.00
Ricks Construction	133,180.00	151	3800.00	2891.00	7682.56	292.00	985.00	3670.00	1376.00	1870.00
Sippel & Adams	152,456.00	300	3432.00	5776.00	2078.44	517.00	1396.00	3656.00	2010.00	2866.00
E. B. Snead	131,478.00	175	1500.00	3200.00	6500.00	436.00	1250.00	3800.00	1686.00	2178.00

Receipt for November 1949 Tabulation of General Bids for Seguin Elementary School. *Author's private collection.*

Front: "Guadalupe County Court House. Seguin, Texas. 9a65-N." *Back*: "Seguin was founded in 1838, and was named in honor Col. Juan N. Seguin, a patriot of the battle of San Jacinto. Its principal industries are pecans, cotton, oil, flour, dairy productions, and hydro-electric power generation. It is noted for its parks and municipally owned utilities. Genuine Curteich-Chicago C.T. American Art: Postcard (Reg. U.S. Pat. Off.)." *Author's private postcard collections.*

BIBLIOGRAPHY

Books

De Cordova, Jacob. *The Texas Immigrant and Traveler's Guide Book.* Austin, TX: De Cordova and Frazier, 1856.

Fitzsimon, Reverend Laurence Julius. *History of Seguin in 1938*, San Antonio, TX: C.H. Jackson Directory Company, 1938.

Gesick, E. John, Jr. *Images of America: Seguin and Guadalupe County*. Charleston, SC: Arcadia Publishing, 2010.

———. *Under the Live Oak Tree*. Seguin, TX: Tommy Brown Printing, 1988.

Gretchen, Mark. *Slave Transactions of Guadalupe County, Texas.* Santa Maria, CA: Janaway Publishing, Inc., 2009.

Jones, Betty Jean. "Joshua and the House He Built." Master's thesis, San Marcos, Southwest Texas State University, 1970.

Moellering, Max Arwerd. *"A History of Guadalupe County, Texas."* Master's thesis, University of Texas–Austin, 1938.

Olmsted, Frederick Law. *A Journey Through Texas; Or, a Saddle-Trip on the Southwestern Frontier*. Austin: University of Texas Press, 1989.

Weinert, Willie Mae. *An Authentic History of Guadalupe County*. Seguin, TX: Seguin Enterprise, 1951.

Williams, Linda, and Bruce Coggin. *McQueeney, Texas: A Pictorial History*. Virginia Beach, VA: Donning Company Publishers, 2011.

BIBLIOGRAPHY

Internet Sources

Ancestry.com. http://www.ancestry.com.
Handbook of Texas Online. http://www.tshaonline.org.
New Braunfels Footprints in Time Historic Walking and Driving Tours. http://nbfootprintsintime.com.
United States Federal Census records. http://www.census.gov.

ABOUT THE AUTHOR

E rin O. Wallace is the published author of *Central Texas Paranormal Society: Their History and Haunted Experiences* and *Haunted New Braunfels: A True Wild West Ghost Town.* With her passion for history and genealogy, she has achieved her goal of being an award-winning syndicated genealogical columnist, a history writer specializing in newspaper and magazine articles and even a museum curator. Wallace has been featured on the Discovery Channel, PBS, *San Antonio Living* TV show, the Emmy-winning *Russell Rush* TV show and numerous independent documentaries and films. Although her love of history and genealogy were her first choices of conversation, speaking of hauntings was never far behind. Having been born to a parent with intense psychic ability, the supernatural was impossible for her to avoid. Her mother had been the subject of study by professors of several universities for ESP and was called on by police departments for assistance for years. Local celebrities and politicians seeking her mother's guidance in their careers were commonplace in Wallace's home. Being involved in paranormal discussions, psychic readings, séances and spirit accounts were a daily occurrence for Wallace from school age to adulthood. Although Wallace did not acquire

Photo by Megan Foster.

her mother's profound psychic abilities, she was blessed with the ability of channeling and sensing the presence of spirits. She has grown comfortable in her ability to recognize what those who have passed wish to express to her and with others. Although she was previously the owner of the SerinGhedi Talent and Social Media Agency, coordinator for Texas Paranormal Events, historical researcher for Gravel Productions, guest coordinator for the Paranormal Mayhem Zone (PMZ) Radio Show, graphic artist, freelance writer and professional genealogical researcher, Wallace has decided to retire. She now focuses on her new marriage and restoring her historical building, the Magnolia Hotel, which she owns with her husband, Jim. To them, it is the most peaceful, tranquil and pleasant place on earth.

MEMORIAL

In memory of my mother, Marguerite "Bubbles" May Nolan Semlinger Wallace (December 15, 1929–February 3, 2014), and my brother, Dave "Davey" Patrick Wallace (December 15, 1951–June 10, 2014). They were born on the same day and then passed away in the same year. They will be deeply missed and forever together.

Visit us at
www.historypress.net
....
This title is also available as an e-book

www.ingramcontent.com/pod-product-compliance
Lightning Source LLC
Chambersburg PA
CBHW060809100426
42813CB00004B/1007